Aldus PageMaker®

Getting Started

**Version 4.0 for use with
Apple® Macintosh® computers**

ALDUS®

FIRST EDITION
January 1990
This manual was created electronically using Aldus® PageMaker® on the Apple® Macintosh® computer. Mechanicals were printed on the Linotronic™ 300 at 2540 dpi, and then reproduced commercially. Art was produced using Aldus FreeHand™ and MacPaint® II, and Capture™.

CREDITS
Installation Guide written by Anne Seeley and edited by Maureen O'Neill
Tutorial written by Carol Brown and edited by Marianne Moon and Margy Kotick
Designed by Olav Martin Kvern and Laura Urban Perry
Illustrated and produced by Joe Friend, D. Reid Johnson, Carl Juarez, Olav Martin Kvern, Arnon Loawhakasetr, Herbert E. Payton, Amy Carroll Porter, Tracy Tobin, Kelli Workman, and Jan C. Wright
Usability testing developed by Brenda Lee Morris

Aldus Corporation	Aldus Europe Limited
411 First Avenue South	Craigcrook Castle
Seattle, WA 98104-2871	Craigcrook Road
USA	Edinburgh, Scotland
Tel. 1 206 622 5500	United Kingdom, EH4 3UH Tel. 44 31 336 1727

If you are outside the U.S. or Canada, please contact your local distributor or dealer.
If you purchased your Aldus software through a hardware manufacturer, technical support for your software may instead be provided as part of the system support from the hardware manufacturer.
ISBN number 1-56026-021-1
Printed in USA

Contents

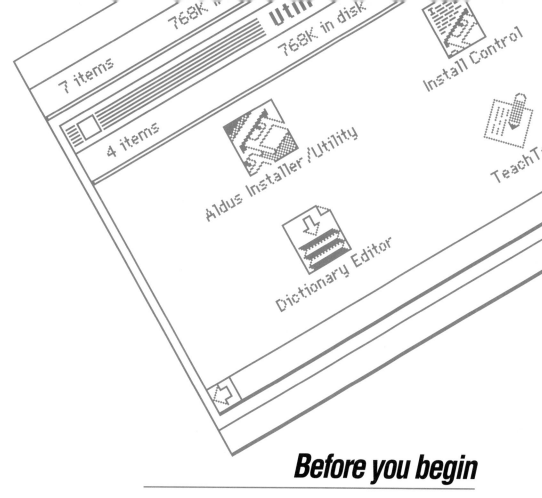

Before you begin

Welcome to Aldus PageMaker 4.0, the only complete writing, editing, design, and production tool for creating professional-quality publications. Whatever your publication requirements, PageMaker 4.0 offers you these key features to help you look your very best in print:

- Powerful word-processing capability

- Sophisticated graphic and typographic controls

- Full capability for long and multi-section publications

- Efficient publication management

About Getting Started

Getting Started is your guide to beginning work with
PageMaker 4.0.

- "Before you begin" tells you what you need to know and
do before you install PageMaker 4.0.

- "Installing PageMaker 4.0" describes how to move the
PageMaker 4.0 files to your hard disk.

- "Learning PageMaker 4.0" includes a selection of tutorial
lessons for a hands-on introduction to the program.

In this section of *Getting Started*, you will find instructions for:

- Checking your PageMaker 4.0 package

- Checking your equipment

- Making a backup copy of the PageMaker 4.0 disk set

- Registering your product

For an illustrated sampler of PageMaker possibilities, refer to
Introduction to PageMaker. For more details about the rest of
the PageMaker manuals, see the list on the next page.

✔ Check your PageMaker package

Whether you have upgraded from an earlier version
of PageMaker or purchased PageMaker 4.0 new, your
PageMaker package includes the following items:

* Four numbered disks

* A license agreement

* A registration card

* Five pieces of printed documentation

    The PageMaker 4.0 documentation provides a variety
    of tools for both new and experienced PageMaker users:

    Getting Started contains everything you need to install and
    learn PageMaker 4.0. In the pocket of *Getting Started,* you
    will find the *Aldus PageMaker 4.0 Quick Reference Guide*, a
    summary of shortcuts and commands, and a Reader Response
    Card, to let us know how we can do better next time.

    Introduction to PageMaker is an illustrated sampler for
    those who are new to desktop publishing in general or to
    PageMaker in particular.

    Aldus PageMaker 4.0 Reference Manual will be your
    companion to PageMaker 4.0 once you have installed the
    program and mastered the basics.

    Templates Guide is a handy guide and reference to the use
    of the model publications, called templates, that you'll find
    in your PageMaker 4.0 package.

    Table Editor Guide is a brief guide to the easy-to-use table
    editor program that is installed with PageMaker 4.0.

    If your package does not include all these items, call Aldus
Customer Relations at (206) 628-2320. If you are outside
the United States or Canada, please contact your local Aldus
distributor or dealer.

✔ Check your equipment

You can use PageMaker 4.0 on any model of Macintosh computer that has a hard disk and a minimum of 1MB memory. To install and run PageMaker 4.0, you must have the following:

Apple System file	Version 6.0.3 (or later)
Apple Finder file	Version 6.1 (or later)
Available memory (RAM)	1MB minimum If you have more than 1MB of memory (at least 2MB is recommended) you can run PageMaker 4.0 under MultiFinder; allocate a minimum of 1.5MB for running PageMaker 4.0 under MultiFinder
Available hard disk space	5MB minimum (if all options are chosen)
Output device	At least one output device driver (such as LaserPrep and LaserWriter) installed, and a corresponding output device (such as a LaserWriter Plus) selected in the Chooser

Before you install PageMaker 4.0, make sure that your hard disk contains only one System folder and that the System folder contains only one System file and one Finder file. Always be sure to use the most recent version of these and other Macintosh System documents.

To use PageMaker 4.0 most effectively, you should be familiar with your Macintosh. Specifically, you should know how to:

- Set up and use your Macintosh, including basic mouse techniques such as pointing, clicking, and dragging

- Select commands from pull-down and pop-up menus

- Work with the Macintosh windows (open, close, scroll, move, resize, and select)

If you are not familiar with these basic tasks, refer to your Macintosh documentation for instructions.

✔ Make a backup copy of the disk set

You must use the Aldus Installer/Utility to install PageMaker 4.0 on your hard disk. Before you do so, make a backup copy of each of the disks in your PageMaker 4.0 package; use these backup disks to install PageMaker 4.0. (Your license agreement authorizes you to make one backup copy of each PageMaker 4.0 disk.)

When making backup copies of the PageMaker 4.0 disks:

• Give the backup disks exactly the same names as the original PageMaker 4.0 disks. Otherwise, when you try to install PageMaker 4.0 from your backup disks, the Installer will not accept them.

• Use the "disk-to-disk" method to copy information from the PageMaker 4.0 disks to the backup disks. For detailed instructions on copying disks, refer to your Macintosh documentation.

The original disks in your PageMaker 4.0 package were locked before shipping. We strongly recommend that you leave them locked to prevent accidental overwriting of the disks or infection by a computer virus. We also recommend that you lock your backup copies before running the Installer.

✔ Register your product

If you have upgraded from an earlier version of PageMaker: You have already registered.

If you purchased a new retail version of PageMaker 4.0: To receive registered customer services, complete and return the registration card you'll find in your PageMaker 4.0 package. If you lose this card, install PageMaker 4.0, then print and use the Registration Card publication that is copied to your hard disk during installation. (Look for it in the Templates folder in the Aldus PageMaker 4.0 folder.)

For additional information on Aldus customer services, refer to the brochure in your product package. ❦

Installing PageMaker 4.0

Many of the PageMaker 4.0 files are compressed to conserve disk space. You must use the Aldus Installer/Utility to decompress the files and transfer them to your hard disk. The Installer is an easy-to-use program that:

* Decompresses and copies the PageMaker 4.0 program and other files from your PageMaker 4.0 disk set to your hard disk.

* Provides ready access during installation to ReadMe and other useful files (described on page 10). Help is available with every Installer screen; simply click the "Help" button for a brief description of what to do next.

* Provides diagnostic tools that can help you or your Technical Support representative if you encounter problems.

In this section of *Getting Started* you will learn how to install Aldus PageMaker 4.0 and related files on your hard disk, and to use the Installer's diagnostic tools to troubleshoot installation or performance of Aldus PageMaker 4.0.

How to install PageMaker 4.0: Summary instructions

Installing PageMaker 4.0 and its related files is a straight-forward procedure, although you have options along the way. The basic steps are listed below. On the next page, you'll find the same procedure described in greater detail and illustrated.

If you're already familiar with the Macintosh, this summary may provide all the information you need. If not, read through the detailed instructions before continuing. Each Installer screen also has a "Help" button; click the "Help" button to display a brief explanation of what to do next.

Note: These instructions assume that you choose to install all the PageMaker 4.0 files. If you do not, the Installer may skip some of the steps listed below.

To install PageMaker 4.0 on your hard disk:

1. **Insert Disk 1 into any disk drive on your Macintosh.**

2. **Double-click the Aldus Installer/Utility icon.**

Aldus Installer/Utility

3. **In the "Aldus Installer Main Window," uncheck any options you do not want to install, then click "Install."**

4. **In the "Aldus APD installation" dialog box, select one or more APD filenames, then click "OK."**

5. **In the "Aldus filter installation" dialog box, select one or more filter filenames, then click "OK."**

6. **In the personalization dialog box, type your name, your company name, and your PageMaker serial number, then click "OK."**

7. **In the "Install files" dialog box, specify where you want the PageMaker 4.0 files to be installed, then click "Install."**

8. **Insert disks as prompted until the installation is complete.**

How to install PageMaker 4.0: Detailed instructions

This section describes the installation process in detail and shows each of the dialog boxes you can expect to see. It also describes the options you have at each step. Remember that the Installer has a "Help" button on every screen; click the "Help" button for onscreen instructions about what to do next.

The Installer automatically copies the PageMaker 4.0 program, the online Help files, the Table Editor, and a number of other files into the Aldus PageMaker 4.0 folder on your hard disk. It also copies the basic spelling and hyphenation dictionaries, the PANTONE® Color library, a folder of Aldus Printer Description files (APDs), a folder of import and export filters, and the Installer itself into the Aldus folder within your System folder. Installing the templates and the sample files for the PageMaker tutorial lessons is optional.

Note: These instructions assume that you choose to install all the PageMaker 4.0 files. If you do not, the Installer may skip some of the steps described below.

To install PageMaker 4.0 on your hard disk:

---

1. Insert Disk 1 into any disk drive on your Macintosh.

Aldus Installer/Utility

2. Double-click the Aldus Installer/Utility icon.
The Installer briefly displays a startup screen, and then displays the "Aldus Installer Main Window."

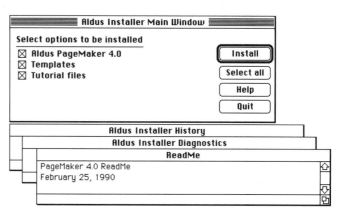

The top half of the screen contains a dialog box where you specify the files you want to install. When the Installer opens, all three options are checked and the "Select all" button is dimmed.

In the lower half of the screen, three text files are displayed; click in the title bar of any of the files to bring it to the front to read. Scroll in the active window to view the entire file.

- ReadMe contains last-minute information about PageMaker 4.0 that became available after the printed documentation went to press. We strongly recommend that you read through this file before continuing with the installation.

- Aldus Installer Diagnostics begins as an empty file. It is where the Installer records the results of the automatic system check that is run by the Installer. If you run any of the utilities from the Diagnostics menu within the Installer, the results of those tests are also recorded in Aldus Installer Diagnostics. For additional information on using the Diagnostics commands, see "More about the Installer," later in this section of *Getting Started*.

- Aldus Installer History also begins as an empty file. When installation begins, the Installer brings this window to the front, where you can watch as it records the copying of files to your hard disk. This record can be helpful later if you need help to resolve a problem with the installation.

These three files are all TeachText files and are saved to the Aldus PageMaker 4.0 folder; you can review them on the screen or print them later using the TeachText application.

3. **Uncheck the options for the files you do not want to install, then click "Install."**

Leave this option checked	To install
Aldus PageMaker 4.0	The PageMaker 4.0 program, the spelling and hyphenation dictionaries, the online Help files, a folder of APD files, a folder of import and export filters, the Installer itself, and miscellaneous related files
Templates	A folder containing the 25 publication templates and 10 grid templates
Tutorial files	A folder of sample files for use in completing the tutorial lessons in *Getting Started*

4. **In the "Aldus APD installation" dialog box, select one or more APD filenames, then click "OK."**

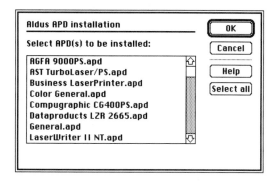

You must install an APD (Aldus Printer Description) file for each printer on which you plan to print publications. Click to select a single file; press the Shift key while clicking to select additional files; click "Select all" to install all the APD files.

5. In the "Aldus filter installation" dialog box, select one or more filter filenames, then click "OK."

```
┌─────────────────────────────────────────────────────┐
│  Aldus Filter installation              ┌──────────┐ │
│                                          │    OK    │ │
│  Select Filter(s) to be installed:      └──────────┘ │
│  ┌──────────────────────────────────┐   ┌──────────┐ │
│  │ Acta Import.flt               ⇧  │   │  Cancel  │ │
│  │ ASCII Text ExportB1.flt          │   └──────────┘ │
│  │ DCA Import B1.flt                │   ┌──────────┐ │
│  │ Mac Word Perfect Import.flt      │   │   Help   │ │
│  │ MS Word 1.05 Import.flt          │   └──────────┘ │
│  │ MS Word 3.0 Import.flt           │   ┌──────────┐ │
│  │ MS Word 3.0/4.0 ExportB2.flt     │   │Select all│ │
│  │ MS Word 4.0 Import B2.flt     ⇩  │   └──────────┘ │
│  └──────────────────────────────────┘                │
│                                                       │
└─────────────────────────────────────────────────────┘
```

You must install an import filter for any word-processing application whose files you expect to use in PageMaker 4.0 publications. Install any export filter, if available, for files that you plan to export from PageMaker 4.0 to your word-processing application. We recommend that you install "Smart ASCII Import.flt," a general-purpose filter for placing any text file.

Click to select a single file; press Shift while clicking to select additional files; click "Select all" to install all the filter files.

Next, the Installer runs one or more system diagnostics and displays the results in the "Aldus Installer Diagnostics" window. This file is saved and can be referred to or printed later using the TeachText application.

Finally, the Installer asks you to personalize your copy of Aldus PageMaker 4.0.

6. Type your name, your company name, and the serial number of your copy of PageMaker, then click "OK."

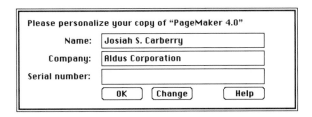

```
┌─────────────────────────────────────────────────────┐
│  Please personalize your copy of "PageMaker 4.0"      │
│                                                       │
│         Name:  ┌──────────────────────────────────┐  │
│                │ Josiah S. Carberry               │  │
│                └──────────────────────────────────┘  │
│      Company:  ┌──────────────────────────────────┐  │
│                │ Aldus Corporation                │  │
│                └──────────────────────────────────┘  │
│ Serial number: ┌──────────────────────────────────┐  │
│                │                                  │  │
│                └──────────────────────────────────┘  │
│       ┌──────┐   ┌────────┐        ┌──────┐           │
│       │  OK  │   │ Change │        │ Help │           │
│       └──────┘   └────────┘        └──────┘           │
└─────────────────────────────────────────────────────┘
```

Press Tab to move from one field to the next within the
dialog box. (Clicking "Cancel" takes you back to the "Aldus
Installer Main Window.")

• **If you have upgraded from an earlier version of PageMaker:**
  Your serial number is the same as for your earlier version.
  You'll find it inside the front cover of your *Aldus
  PageMaker 3.0 User Manual*, on your original
  PageMaker Program Disk, on the bottom of the box in
  which you received your original PageMaker package, or
  on the mailing label of your PageMaker 4.0 upgrade
  package.

• **If you purchased a new retail PageMaker 4.0 package:** Look
  for your serial number on the registration card flyer in
  your product package, or on the bottom of the box.

The Installer requires that you type something in every
field on this screen. The serial number must have exactly the
same format as your PageMaker serial number. Type all the
numbers and hyphens, but exclude any letters you may find
at the beginning of the number.

After you click "OK," the Installer asks you to verify
what you just typed.

```
┌─────────────────────────────────────────────────┐
│                                                   │
│  Confirm your personalization information:        │
│                                                   │
│         Name:   Josiah S. Carberry                │
│                                                   │
│      Company:   Aldus Corporation                 │
│                                                   │
│  Serial number:                                   │
│                  ┌──── OK ────┐  ┌─ Change ─┐     │
│                  └────────────┘  └──────────┘     │
└─────────────────────────────────────────────────┘
```

Click "Change" to return to the personalization dialog
box to make corrections, or click "OK" to continue the
installation.

The Installer checks to make sure that you have enough
free disk space, and then asks where you want to install
PageMaker 4.0. The space check is performed automatically
on your startup hard disk. If you plan to install PageMaker
4.0 on a separate hard disk, check for space on that disk by
clicking the "Drive" button when the Installer displays the
next dialog box.

7. **In the "Install files" dialog box, specify where you want the PageMaker 4.0 files to be installed, then click "Install."**

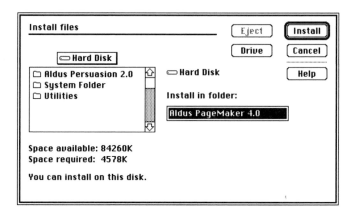

If sufficient disk space is available, specify where you want PageMaker 4.0 to be installed. The default is a folder called Aldus PageMaker 4.0 on your hard disk.

If disk space is insufficient, click "Cancel" to return to the Installer startup screen. There you can either choose fewer files to install, or click "Quit" to return to your Macintosh desktop and remove other files from your hard disk before starting the Installer again.

8. **Insert disks as prompted.**

The Installer asks you to insert each of the four disks in turn, or as many as are necessary for the files you want to install. You can insert any disk in any of the disk drives on your Macintosh.

The "Aldus Installer History" window comes to the front, so you can watch what is happening as installation proceeds.

When the Installer has finished, it briefly displays a final alert box. Click "OK," or simply wait five seconds for it to disappear automatically. The Installer returns you to the Macintosh desktop.

What the Installer installs

If you install all the PageMaker 4.0 files, you'll find the following folders and files on your hard disk.

In the PageMaker 4.0 folder (or whatever folder you specified during installation), you'll find:

Folder/File	Description
Aldus Installer Diagnostics	A TeachText file containing the results of any tests run during installation
Aldus Installer History[1]	A TeachText file containing a history of the installation
Kern Tracks	A file containing custom track-kerning information used by PageMaker 4.0—if you modify, move, or delete this file, PageMaker will use its default kerning information
PageMaker 4.0	The PageMaker 4.0 program
PM4 Help	The file containing PageMaker 4.0's context-sensitive online Help
ReadMe	A TeachText file containing last-minute product information that became available after the printed documentation went to press
Table Editor	A program that lets you create and edit complex tables for placing in PageMaker publications
Templates	A folder containing the PageMaker 4.0 templates (installed only if you chose the "Templates" option in the main window of the Installer), as well as several miscellaneous small files including the online Registration Card
Tutorial	A folder containing files for the tutorial lessons (installed only if you chose the "Tutorial files" option in the main window of the Installer)

[1] Aldus Installer History records the history of your PageMaker 4.0 installation and contains valuable information for troubleshooting problems you may encounter when installing or using PageMaker 4.0. Aldus Installer History contains the date and time of the installation; a list of all files installed, including the folders they were installed in and the disk they were installed from; and a list of any errors the Installer encountered.

In the System folder, you'll find:

Folder/File	Description
PM4 Defaults	A file containing the default settings that come with PageMaker 4.0
PM4 RSRC	A file containing language-dependent information required for your version of PageMaker 4.0—if you modify, move, or delete this file, you will not be able to run PageMaker 4.0

In the Aldus folder within your System folder, you'll find:

Folder/File	Description
Aldus Filters	A folder containing text import and export filters used by PageMaker to place and export text
Aldus Prep	A file containing Aldus' custom PostScript dictionary that works with PageMaker's printer driver (this should be the only copy of Aldus Prep on your Macintosh)
APDs	A folder containing printer information files
Proximity	A folder containing the dictionary files for the language(s)
PANTONE Colors	A file containing the PANTONE® Color library for use by PageMaker 4.0 and other Aldus applications
Utilities	A folder containing a copy of the Aldus Installer/Utility, and TeachText (the application that allows you to read the Aldus Installer Diagnostics, Aldus Installer History, and ReadMe files)

The Aldus folder contains files that may be shared among Aldus applications. If the Aldus folder already exists when you install PageMaker 4.0, the necessary files are added to it; if the Aldus folder does not already exist, the Installer creates it.

Important: Because the Aldus folder contains files that are needed for optimal operation and performance of PageMaker 4.0 and other applications, we strongly recommend that you not move, rename, or delete the folder and that you not move, rename, or delete any of the files or folders within it. You may open the Utilities folder to run any of the programs installed there, but should not modify any of the other files in any way.

Notes on adding and replacing dictionaries

Each PageMaker 4.0 package comes with a set of dictionary files for one language. These dictionaries are used for hyphenation and spellchecking within PageMaker 4.0. Additional dictionary packages are available from Aldus Corporation; outside the United States and Canada, contact your Aldus dealer or distributor.

* When you install PageMaker 4.0 for the first time, the language that came with your version of the product is installed automatically.

* When you install additional languages from one of the separate language packs, a dialog box appears with two list boxes. One box shows the language(s) already installed; another list box shows what additional languages may be installed at this time.

* If you re-install PageMaker 4.0 at any time, the same dialog box appears, whether or not you have installed additional language dictionaries.

For more information about installing and re-installing multiple language dictionary sets, refer to the information that comes with any Aldus dictionaries you may purchase. For more information about dictionaries, hyphenation, and spellchecking in general, refer to the *Aldus PageMaker 4.0 Reference Manual.*

Notes for users of earlier versions of PageMaker

PageMaker 4.0 is installed in its own folder on your hard disk; you can keep the PageMaker 3.0 folder on your hard disk as well. If you have both a version of PageMaker 3.0 (3.0, 3.01, 3.02, 3.02CE, or 3.5) and PageMaker 4.0 on your hard disk, double-clicking a PageMaker 3.0 file opens your version of PageMaker 3.0; double-clicking a PageMaker 4.0 file opens PageMaker 4.0.

If you delete the PageMaker 3.0 program, you must open PageMaker 4.0 and use the "Open..." command to open and convert a PageMaker 3.0 file. The file will automatically open and convert as an untitled copy of the original. Use the "Save" or "Save as..." command to save the converted copy as a PageMaker 4.0 publication.

Although you can convert PageMaker 3.0 publications to PageMaker 4.0 publications, the conversion may cause subtle changes to the publication (for example, recomposition of the text, so that line breaks may be different). Because of this, you may wish to complete existing PageMaker 3.0 projects in PageMaker 3.0 and to begin all new projects in PageMaker 4.0. When all 3.0 projects are completed, you can remove PageMaker 3.0 from your computer.

For a full discussion of all the issues to consider when converting 3.0 publications to 4.0, refer to the article, "Converting and transferring PageMaker publications," in the *Aldus PageMaker 4.0 Reference Manual*.

More about the Installer

The Aldus Installer is a useful, multi-purpose program. Use it to install PageMaker 4.0 or to run system tests that may help explain performance problems.

• To start the Installer, double-click the Installer icon on your backup copy of PageMaker 4.0 Disk 1.

• To decompress and install any file you chose not to install originally (for example, the templates or tutorial files), insert the appropriate backup disk into any drive on your Macintosh, then double-click the icon for the file you want.

• To run any of the diagnostic tests after installing PageMaker 4.0, look for the Installer in the Utilities folder (inside the Aldus folder in your System folder). Double-click the Installer icon to start the program.

The rest of this section provides a brief reference to three Installer menus: File, Diagnostics, and Windows.

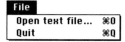

File menu

Command	What it does
"Open text file…"	Lets you open any TeachText file on your system while you are in the Installer.
"Quit"	Lets you quit the Installer at any time from any point in the installation process.

Diagnostics menu

The Diagnostics menu provides access to nine programs that run different kinds of tests on your Macintosh. The Installer runs one or more of the tests as part of the installation process. You can choose from the Diagnostics menu on your own any time. A technical support representative may also ask you to run one or more when trying to help solve a problem.

When you run any of the diagnostics, the Installer displays the results in the "Aldus Installer Diagnostics" window. This window contains a TeachText file that is automatically saved when you leave the Installer. To review or print the file in TeachText, double-click its icon. The history of diagnostics run during installation is saved in the PageMaker 4.0 folder. The history of diagnostics you may run later is saved in your top-level directory and is overwritten each time you run diagnostics.

Command	What it does
"Run all diagnostics"	Runs all nine tests in sequence.
"System configuration"	Checks to see what type of machine you are using, the System version, available memory, and current printer and version. This test runs automatically as part of the installation process.
"Check for multiple System and Finder files"	Checks to see that you have only one System file and one Finder file on your machine, and tells you where they are located.

Command	What it does (continued)
"Check for APDs and Aldus Prep"	Checks to see that you have only one set of printer description files and one Aldus Prep file on your machine, and tells you where they are located.
"List INITs, CDEVs, and RDEVs"	Checks for and displays a list of any of these three types of startup files that you may have installed on your Macintosh. This information can be useful to a technician helping you with performance or memory problems you may encounter while using PageMaker 4.0.
"Check for damaged fonts"	Checks for and displays a list of any fonts in your System that are damaged and need to be replaced.
"Check for duplicate font IDs"	Checks for and displays a list of any fonts in your System that have duplicate identification numbers (which can be the cause of display or printing problems).
"Check for other Aldus applications"	Checks for and displays a list of other Aldus applications you may have installed on your Macintosh.
"Check for import/export filters"	Checks to see what import or export filters are installed on your Macintosh.
"Check installed language files"	Checks to see that all the necessary dictionary files for each installed language are in the Language folder within the Aldus folder.

```
Windows
✓Aldus Installer Main Window
✓ReadMe
✓Aldus Installer Diagnostics
✓Aldus Installer History
```

Windows menu

The Windows menu lists all currently open files. Initially, the list consists of the names of the files that are automatically opened when you start the Installer. If you open any additional TeachText files while using the Installer, their names also appear on the Windows menu. Selecting any item brings its window to the front. ❦

Learning PageMaker 4.0

Learning a computer program is something like learning how to swim. Some people take classes. Others jump right in, splashing around until they eventually get the hang of it. Still others wade in gradually with a companion who can give them guidance and reassurance. This book is your companion and guide to PageMaker 4.0.

What's in these lessons

The tutorial is divided into three sections and is actually three tutorials in one:

- "Getting down to basics"

- "Producing a newsletter": Lessons 1 through 4

- "Practice Topics": "Setting indents and tabs" and "Unraveling threaded text."

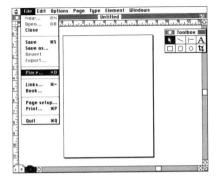

Getting down to basics

"Basics" is a gently guided tour through the fundamental tools and techniques you'll work with in PageMaker and includes opportunities just to "play around."

Producing a newsletter: Lessons 1 through 4

There is no better way to learn PageMaker than to use it to produce a publication. In these four lessons you will create a two-page newsletter. At the same time, you'll become familiar with the essential concepts and skills you'll need to produce your own work: You'll learn how to place and integrate text and graphics on a page, move them and change their size, edit and format text, and print.

All the text you place in the newsletter was created in Microsoft® Word 4.0. The graphics were prepared in MacPaint®, Aldus® FreeHand™, and ImageStudio™. Some of the titles were formatted in Helvetica® and the remaining titles and body text in Times® Roman.

Newsletter: master page

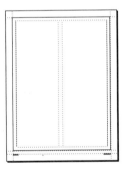

Lesson 1 shows you how to set up a master page in preparation for laying out the newsletter.

Newsletter: beginning page 1

Lesson 2 leads you through the layout of three elements on the first page of the newsletter: the masthead, the lead story, and a graphic image at the top of the page.

Newsletter: completed page 1

Lesson 3 shows you how to finish the first page of the newsletter: You'll use PageMaker's new story editor to edit a table ("A Brief History of Publishing"), place it in the newsletter, and place a box around the table with a shadow behind it.

Newsletter: completed page 2

Lesson 4 shows you how to produce the second page of the newsletter. You'll use styles, which make formatting more efficient, and put the finishing touches on your publication before printing it. This lesson also asks you to repeat some things you've already mastered, such as placing graphic images and laying out the second story. It takes a slightly different approach from that of earlier lessons: It outlines the general steps you'll follow rather than giving you the details. However, there are plenty of cross-references to help you if you make a mistake or forget how to do something.

Practice topics

When you have had some experience using PageMaker on your own and are ready to learn more, you may want to try these lessons. The focus in these lessons is on experimentation rather than on creating a publication.

Setting indents and tabs. If you're accustomed to using the spacebar to line up text on the page and have had some surprises, you'll want to get into the habit of using the Tab key and setting tab stops and indents using the "Indents/tabs..." command on the Type menu. In this lesson, you'll experiment with setting a variety of indents and tab stops and then test your understanding by creating a bulleted list.

Unraveling threaded text. This lesson elaborates on one of the most fundamental concepts in PageMaker: how text flows from text block to text block. Simple enough on the surface, text flow is a powerful feature that lets you break a single story into as many blocks as you need while keeping the flow of the story from block to block intact. You'll practice adding text within a story and outside it, deleting text, breaking text blocks apart, combining them, and reorganizing them.

How to use this tutorial

The goal of this tutorial is to present basic PageMaker concepts and to guide you through some techniques so you can begin to use PageMaker 4.0 immediately and to your best advantage.

To make your learning easier, we've sprinkled "On your own" sections throughout. Use them to test your understanding of specific concepts and their integration with others you've already learned. Look, too, for the "◆" that marks the hints if you make a mistake or forget how to do something. And, if you're working with Lessons 1 through 4 but don't want to try each lesson, you'll find the publication completed for Lessons 1, 2, and 3 in the Tutorial folder. For example, if you want to try only Lesson 3, you can open the file called "Lesson 2 done" and proceed without having to first complete Lessons 1 and 2.

There are several ways you may use this tutorial, depending on how you learn best and on your experience with desktop publishing and PageMaker.

If you are new to desktop publishing and PageMaker, there are a couple of approaches you can take depending on how you learn best. If you're most comfortable with step-by-step instructions, you may benefit most by starting with "Getting down to basics" and proceeding through to the end of the four newsletter project lessons. If you learn best by experimentation, step through the "Basics" lesson and then try using PageMaker to produce a publication of your own. You can always dip back into the tutorial to pick up techniques you need. Try the practice topics, too, though you may want to explore these subjects after you've had some experience using PageMaker.

If you are an experienced user of other desktop publishing programs, but new to PageMaker, you may find it most helpful to work through "Getting down to basics" and then to skim through the newsletter project, practicing the features that are new to you. You might want to try your hand at the "Practice topics," too, as these give you a glimpse at how PageMaker handles indents, tabs, and the flow of text between text blocks.

If you are an experienced user of earlier versions of PageMaker, you'll want to try the features of the new story editor used in Lessons 3 and 4. Take a look at the practice lessons on setting indents and tabs, as PageMaker 4.0 works a bit differently from earlier versions. And if you've never quite mastered the complexities of threaded text, you may want to try the practice lesson, "Unraveling threaded text."

Before you plunge in...

For everyone

Before you begin, we assume you've installed PageMaker. If you haven't, follow the directions in "Installing PageMaker 4.0" earlier in this book.

Also, we assume you know the Macintosh basics, including how to:

* Find your way around the desktop

* Click, double-click, press, and drag using the mouse

* Move about on the screen, including the use of scroll bars

* Choose from menus and dialog boxes

* Locate, open, copy, delete, close, print, and save documents

If these techniques are unfamiliar to you and you'd like some training, refer to the tutorial, "Learning Macintosh Basics," in the *Macintosh System Software User's Guide* that came with your Macintosh computer.

For users of the International English and Canadian English product

The practice publications in this book are designed to be reproduced on either U.S. letter paper or international A-4 paper; the instructions apply to both sizes of document. Use the inch measurement to produce a U.S. letter-size document. Use the metric measurements shown in parentheses to produce an A4 document; they do not provide a direct conversion from inches to the metric system, but are adapted to work well on A4 size pages. If you're using the International English version of PageMaker 4.0, there may be occasional differences between the sample screens printed in this book and the screens as they appear on your computer. If you're using the Canadian English version of PageMaker 4.0, your product defaults are set for U.S. letter-size paper.

Getting out of trouble...

If you run into problems using PageMaker 4.0, you'll find the new online Help useful. It's organized into two categories: "Commands" and "Topics." "Commands" gives you information about all the commands on all the menus; "Topics" gives you information on a variety of subjects that may concern you.

If you are stymied by a problem and do not know how to proceed, the solution may be only a few keystrokes away. Choose "Help" from the Windows menu and then select "Topics" from the window that appears. Scroll through the list until you find the topic "Troubleshooting." When you look at that topic, you'll find a set of steps to help you get past the obstacle.

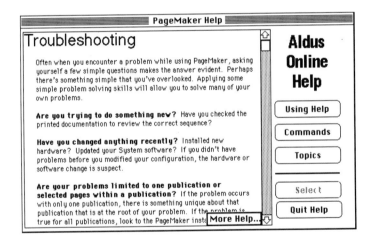

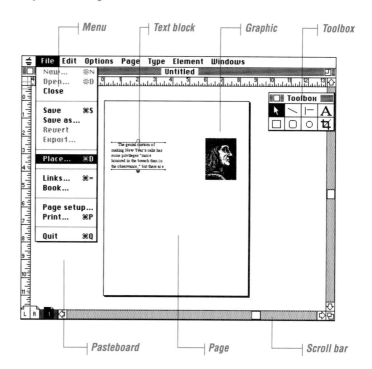

Getting down to basics

"Getting down to basics" presents opportunities for you to use the fundamental tools and techniques you will need to work with PageMaker 4.0, rather than concentrating on creating a product such as a newsletter or a brochure. (You'll do that in later lessons.)

Use "Getting down to basics" as an opportunity to experiment; *don't worry about making mistakes.* If at any time you become confused or lost, start a section over and try again. Or refer to the notes marked with a small ◆. The notes give information that may help you undo a mistake or remind you of a technique you may have forgotten. Above all, remember that the more time you take to experiment with the different features and commands introduced in this lesson, the faster you'll learn PageMaker 4.0.

In this lesson you'll learn how to:

- Start PageMaker and begin a publication

- Recognize the publication window and use PageMaker's tools

- Place a graphic image or a block of text

- Move text or a graphic on the page

- Change the size of a graphic or a block of text

- Undo mistakes

- Edit and format text

- Save and close your PageMaker publication

What's in this lesson

Starting PageMaker

Begin by starting PageMaker. The PageMaker application should be located in the PageMaker 4.0 folder. You start it as you would any Macintosh application: Open the folder with PageMaker in it and double-click the PageMaker 4.0 application icon.

1. Double-click the PageMaker 4.0 folder to open it.

◆ If you cannot locate the PageMaker 4.0 folder, look in another likely folder, such as Applications, and open that. Also, depending on how your desktop is set up, you may see a list of names rather than an icon.

2. Double-click the PageMaker 4.0 icon to start PageMaker.

❶ *Open the PageMaker 4.0 folder.*

❷ *Double-click the PageMaker 4.0 icon.*

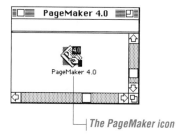

└─│ *The PageMaker icon*

Starting a new publication

As with any other Macintosh application, you create a document using the "New…" command from the File menu.

1. Choose "New…" from the File menu.
When you choose the "New…" command, PageMaker displays the "Page setup" dialog box. This is where you specify the page and printing options for your publication: for example, the page size, the orientation (tall or wide), double-sided or facing pages, margins, and so on.

2. In the "Page setup" dialog box, make sure the "Letter" (A4) and "Tall" options are selected.
If these options are not selected, choose "Letter" (A4) from the "Page" pop-up menu and click the "Tall" button.

➊ *Choose "New…"*

➋ *Select the "Tall" and "Letter" options.*

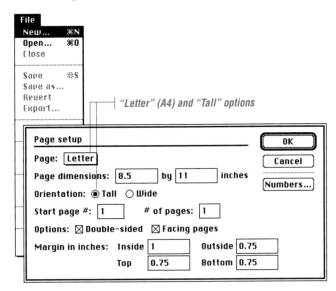

─┤ *"Letter" (A4) and "Tall" options*

3. Click "OK."
This sets up a letter-size (or A4 size) page with a vertical orientation.

➌ *Click "OK."*

Exploring the pasteboard

When you create a publication, PageMaker displays an empty page centered on the pasteboard. The page and pasteboard are where you lay out the text and graphics of your publication. The idea of using a pasteboard is nothing new; graphic artists have been using pasteboards for years. What makes PageMaker's page and pasteboard different is that they're on your computer screen, and all the tools you need to lay out your page are a mouse-click away.

Take a few minutes to familiarize yourself with PageMaker's pasteboard and window.

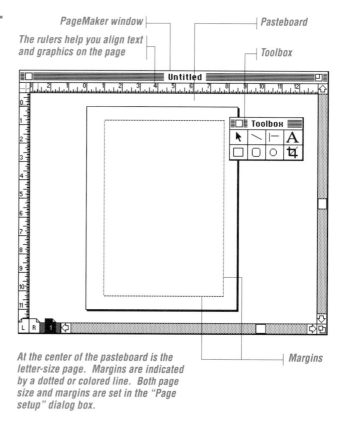

PageMaker window | *Pasteboard*

The rulers help you align text and graphics on the page | *Toolbox*

At the center of the pasteboard is the letter-size page. Margins are indicated by a dotted or colored line. Both page size and margins are set in the "Page setup" dialog box. | *Margins*

The toolbox

The icons in the toolbox represent the tools you use in PageMaker. Try these tools out now, particularly the drawing tools. If the toolbox restricts your view of your work, move it by dragging its title bar.

Before continuing with the lesson, you may want to remove everything you added. To do this quickly, select the pointer tool and choose "Select all" from the Edit menu. Then press the Delete key.

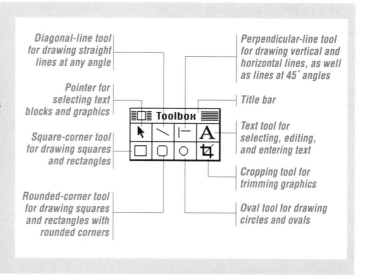

Diagonal-line tool for drawing straight lines at any angle

Perpendicular-line tool for drawing vertical and horizontal lines, as well as lines at 45° angles

Pointer for selecting text blocks and graphics

Title bar

Square-corner tool for drawing squares and rectangles

Text tool for selecting, editing, and entering text

Cropping tool for trimming graphics

Rounded-corner tool for drawing squares and rectangles with rounded corners

Oval tool for drawing circles and ovals

Experimenting with graphics

The idea behind desktop publishing is simple: Take text and graphics that have been created on a computer and combine them into a single publication that can be formatted, resized, and printed to produce professional-quality pages.

You put text and graphics into your PageMaker publication by using one of the most important commands in PageMaker, the "Place..." command. In this example you'll place an image of Aldus Manutius on the page. (Aldus Manutius was the founder of a great 15th-century publishing house, the Aldine Press.) Then you'll experiment with moving the graphic around the pasteboard and with changing its size. If you need more information on working with graphics, refer to the article "Working with graphics" in the *Aldus PageMaker 4.0 Reference Manual.*

The place icons

After you select the "Place..." command and click "OK," PageMaker loads the pointer with a copy of the text or graphics file, and the pointer then changes to one of the icons shown here.

 For text when autoflow is turned off

 For text when autoflow is turned on

 For one page of text when autoflow is turned on

 For paint-type (bitmapped) graphics

 For draw-type (object-oriented) graphics

 For Scrapbook images; the number indicates how many images there are

 For scanned images created in TIFF (tag image file format)

 For images created in EPS (Encapsulated PostScript) format

Placing a graphic image

1. **Choose "Place..." from the File menu.**

2. **In the "Place document" dialog box, double-click to open the Tutorial folder, and double-click again to open the Basics Lesson folder. Double-click "Practice graphic."**

   This is the first of several files that have been prepared and stored on the disk for your use. The graphic image was created with MacPaint and then stored on disk.

   ◆ If you don't see the Tutorial folder, the files may be in another folder. Use "Find File" in the Apple menu to search for "Practice graphic," or check with the person who installed PageMaker on your computer to help you find them. Make a note in the margin so when you want to retrieve files later in these lessons, you'll remember where to find them.

3. **Position the loaded text icon at the center of the page and click.**

❶ *Choose "Place..." from the File menu.*

❷ *Open the Tutorial and the Basics Lesson folder double-click "Practice graphic."*

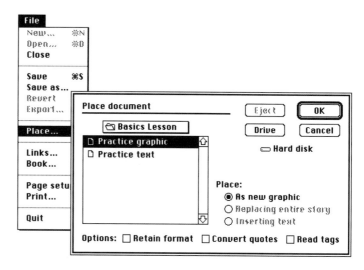

❸ *Position the icon at the center the page and click.*

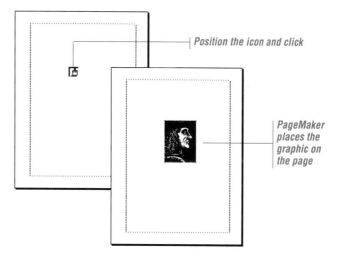

Position the icon and click

PageMaker places the graphic on the page

Moving a graphic around the pasteboard

Just as you can move graphics and text on a conventional pasteboard, you can move what you place in PageMaker simply by dragging. Take a few moments to experiment with moving the graphic around the page and pasteboard.

1. **Make sure the graphic is still selected.**
   You can tell the graphic is selected when PageMaker displays square handles around it. If you do not see any handles, the graphic is deselected. To select the graphic, move the pointer anywhere inside the graphic (not on its edges) and click.

   To deselect the graphic, move the pointer outside the graphic and click. The selection handles disappear.

① *Click inside the graphic with the pointer tool.*

Selection handles around the graphic indicate it has been selected

2. **Point anywhere inside the graphic and hold down the mouse button until you see a four-headed arrow. Then, without letting go, drag the graphic to a new position.**
   Don't worry at this point if you changed the size or shape of the graphic. You'll adjust it later.

◆ Did PageMaker display an empty box when you moved the graphic? Don't worry. It just means you moved the graphic faster than your computer could redraw it. When you stop dragging, PageMaker displays the image.

② *Point anywhere inside the graphic and hold down the mouse button...*

...until the pointer changes to a four-headed arrow. Then drag the graphic to a new position.

◆ If you want to start over, select the graphic image. Choose "Place…" from the File menu, open "Practice graphic" again, and click "Replacing entire graphic." Click "OK." PageMaker removes the graphic on the page and replaces it with the graphic from the disk.

Undoing mistakes

One of the handiest commands in PageMaker is "Undo" on the Edit menu. The "Undo" command records your last action and gives you the option of changing your mind. You must, however, choose "Undo" before taking any other action.

Try this example:

1. **Hold the mouse button down and move the graphic on the page.**

2. **Choose "Undo move" from the Edit menu.** The graphic returns to its original location. "Undo" does not undo every action in PageMaker, but you'll find it a good place to begin. When you cannot undo an action, "Cannot undo" is dimmed on the Edit menu. For more about "Undo," refer to the "Undo" command description in the *Aldus PageMaker 4.0 Reference Manual*.

❶ Hold the mouse button down and drag the graphic on the page.

❷ Choose "Undo move" from the Edit menu.

Command name changes to indicate the last action

Changing the size of a graphic

When you want to change the size of
a graphic, drag a square handle.

1. **Using the pointer, select the graphic
    (if it is not already selected).**

    Using the pointer, select the graphic.

2. **Drag any square handle and experiment
    with sizing the graphic.**
    Watch how the shape changes
    depending on whether you drag a top,
    bottom, or side handle. Try sizing the
    graphic proportionally by holding
    down the Shift key as you drag.

    Drag any square handle to resize the graphic.

|—| *Handles*

3. **When you finish experimenting, return the
    graphic to its approximate original size.**
    Then move it near the top of the page
    to get ready to place text in upcoming
    steps.

    *Return the graphic to its
    approximate original size.*

◆   If you have seriously distorted the
    original image and you want to restore
    it to its original proportions (though
    not its original size), first select the
    graphic. Then press the Shift key
    while you drag a square handle
    to resize.

Viewing the page

As you work with PageMaker, you'll often change the display size of the page. PageMaker has seven different page display sizes and which one you choose depends on what you're doing. Close-up page display sizes ("Actual size," "200% size," and "400% size") are useful for doing detailed work, while smaller ones ("Fit in window," "25% size," "50% size," and "75% size") are for seeing the big picture.

You'll find three page display sizes to be the most useful. So far, you've been working in the "Fit in window" size, which is handy for checking the overall composition of your page. To edit text, however, you'll want to zoom in to "Actual size" so you can see what you're editing. And you'll find "200% size" helpful when precision is imperative.

There are two ways to change page display sizes. You can choose commands from the Page menu or you can use the keyboard. Use the menu when you don't need to zoom to a specific part of the page; use the keyboard when you want to zoom to a particular point. The latter method is the one we suggest you use in these lessons.

If you need more information on viewing the page, refer to the article "Moving around in your publication" and the "Actual size" (% size) command description in the *Aldus PageMaker 4.0 Reference Manual.*

"Actual size"

"200% size"

Using the Page menu

To zoom to "Actual size":

1. **Choose "Actual size" from the Page menu.**
   Depending on the size of your monitor, you may not see the whole page. But you'll notice the image is larger and that you can see more detail.

◆ If the page display size did not change at all, you were already in "Actual size." Proceed to Step 2 to see a difference.

◆ If the graphic image disappeared from view, don't panic. Use the scroll bars in the window to move the page around until you locate the image again. To move a short distance, click the arrows at the ends of the scroll bars; to move a greater distance, click the gray portion of the scroll bar or move the white scroll boxes in the scroll bars.

2. **To return to the page display size that fits in the window, choose "Fit in window" from the Page menu.**

① *Choose "Actual size" from the Page menu.*

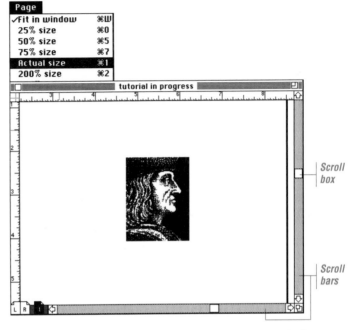

Scroll box

Scroll bars

"Actual size"

② *To return to the previous view choose "Fit in window."*

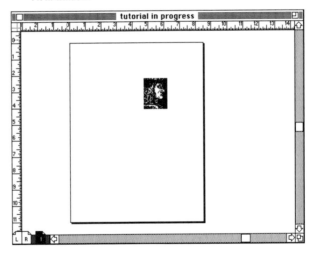

"Fit in window"

Using the keyboard

Using the keyboard is efficient because you can control what part of the publication you zoom to. We recommend that you use these keyboard shortcuts whenever you change page display sizes in this tutorial.

For example, to move quickly between "Fit in window" and "Actual size":

1. **Position the pointer in the top-left corner of the graphic, hold down the Option + Command keys and click.**
   This zooms you into the top-left corner of the graphic in "Actual size."

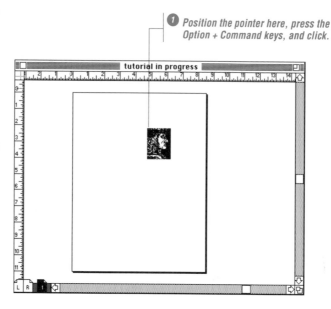

① *Position the pointer here, press the Option + Command keys, and click.*

"Fit in window"

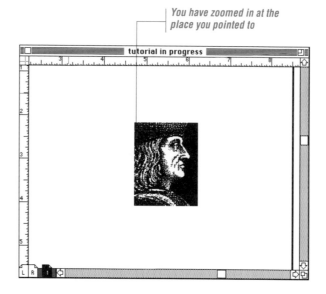

You have zoomed in at the place you pointed to

"Actual size"

2. **To return to "Fit in window" page display size, press Option + Command and click again.**

② *Press Option + Command and click again.*

On your own
Changing page display sizes using the keyboard

Experiment with changing page display sizes:

1. **To start, point anywhere in the graphic.**

2. **Hold down the Option + Command keys and click. (To zoom from "Fit in window" or "Actual size" to "200% size," press the Shift key along with the Option + Command keys.)**

3. **Move the pointer to different areas of the graphic and zoom from one display size to another by trying each combination of the keys shown below.**

When you finish, return to the "Fit in window" page display size before going on to the next section.

For more information on changing page display sizes, refer to the article "Moving around in your publication" in the *Aldus PageMaker 4.0 Reference Manual*.

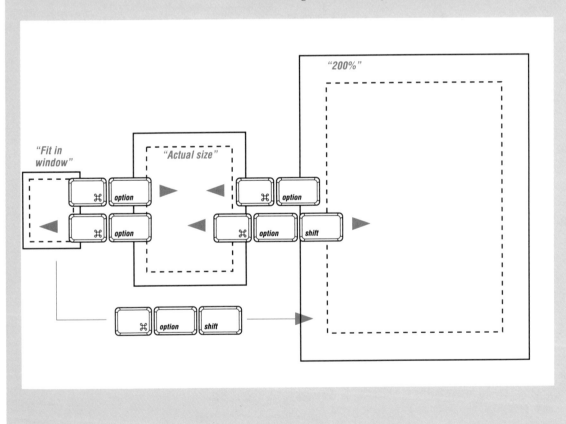

Editing and formatting text

The ability to format text is a cornerstone of graphic design. PageMaker gives you remarkable control over all facets of type including the typeface, its size, spacing, alignment on the page, and so on. For a sense of how easy it is to work with text in PageMaker, you'll place some text, then edit and format it.

Placing a text file

Placing text in PageMaker is similar to placing a graphic. In this example, you'll place the text file, "Practice text," on the page.

1. **Choose "Place..." from the File menu.**

2. **In the "Place document" dialog box, double click to open the Tutorial folder and double-click again to open the Basics Lesson folder. Then double-click "Practice text."**
   The icon changes to indicate the kind of file you are placing. In this case, you've selected a text file, so the pointer changes to a loaded text icon, but no text will appear until you click the icon in the next step.

❶ *Choose "Place..." from the File menu.*

❷ *Open the Tutorial folder and the Basics Lesson folder. Double-click "Practice text."*

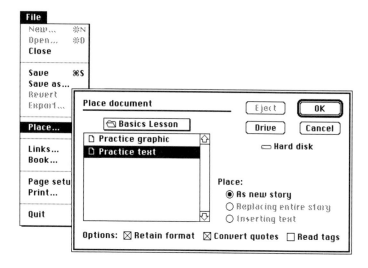

3. Position the loaded text icon just below the Aldus graphic and click.

The size of your screen determines to some extent how PageMaker displays type. So you will either see small type as gray lines or you may be able to see the letters and words (as shown). To see the text in more detail, zoom in for a close-up display size.

◆ If you didn't place the text just where you want it, you can move it. Using the pointer, point anywhere inside the text block and hold down the mouse button until you see a four-headed arrow. Then, without letting go, drag the graphic to a new position.

◆ If the text block is too narrow, you can drag a square corner out to make the text block larger.

③ *Position the loaded text icon just below the Aldus graphic and click.*

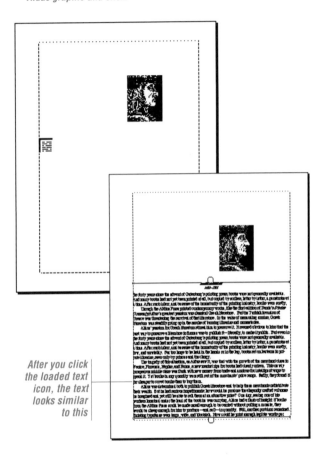

After you click the loaded text icon, the text looks similar to this

When to use the text and pointer tools

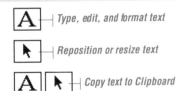

It is useful to note that when you work with the *content* of a text block—inserting, deleting, or formatting text—you use the text tool. When you manipulate the text block as an *object*—to move the block or size it, for example—you use the pointer tool just as you would to manipulate a graphic. You can use either tool to copy text to the Clipboard (a temporary holding place where PageMaker stores text or graphics you cut or copy) for insertion on another page or into another publication.

Editing text

This section of the lesson gives you the opportunity to edit text using the text tool, which is useful for making minor changes.

Inserting text

Start by making sure you are in "Actual size" so the text is large enough to read and edit easily. If you can read the text already, omit Step 1 and proceed to Step 2.

1. **Position the pointer in the middle of the top line of text, hold down the Option + Command keys, and click.**
   Remember that where you point as you press these keys determines what portion of the text you will see when you zoom to "Actual size."

❶ Hold down Option + Command and click in the top line of the text.

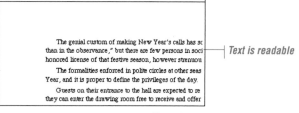

Text is readable

"Actual size"

2. **Select the text tool.**
   When you select the text tool and move it to the page, it takes the shape of an I-beam.

❷ Select the text tool.

After you select the text tool, the cursor becomes an I-beam

3. **Using the text tool, click anywhere in the text.**
   When you click, the I-beam changes to a blinking insertion point, indicating that PageMaker is ready for you to type and edit text.

❸ Click where you want to edit.

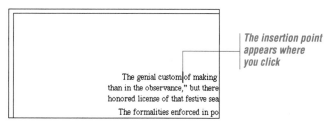

The insertion point appears where you click

4. Practice typing and inserting text on the page.

You insert text in much the same way as in a word-processing program: Click the insertion point where you want to insert text, and type.

◆ You can undo any editing by choosing "Undo edit" from the Edit menu before taking any other action.

Deleting text

Before you can delete text, you must select it. (You must also select text—or at the least have an insertion point in the text—before you can format it.)

1. Drag the mouse over a portion of text to select it, just as you would in a word-processing program.

2. Choose "Cut" from the Edit menu.

This removes whatever is selected.

3. Restore the edited text by choosing "Paste" from the Edit menu.

◆ If you want to start over, select the text block using the pointer. Choose "Place…" from the File menu. Select "Practice text" again and click "Replacing entire story." Click "OK." As with the graphic, PageMaker removes the text and replaces it.

④ *Practice typing and inserting text on the page.*

① *Select a portion of the text.*

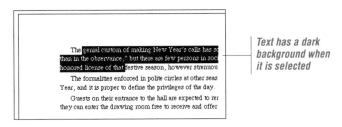

Text has a dark background when it is selected

② *Choose "Cut."*   ③ *Choose "Paste."*

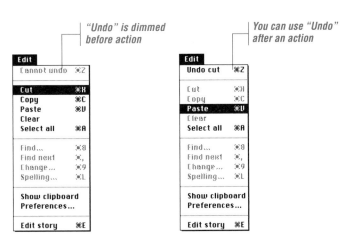

Formatting text

For the most part, the formats you apply in a word-processing program will be retained when you place the document in PageMaker. You can also change and refine the formats using the commands on the Type menu. You might alter the size and style of the type or the alignment of a paragraph, for example.

On your own
Selecting text

Double-click to select a word

The genial custom of making New Year's calls has some privileges "more honored in the breach than in the observance," but there are few persons in society who would wish to abolish the time-honored license of that festive season, however strenuously they may counsel wise reforms.

The formalities enforced in polite circles at other seasons are relaxed with the coming of the New Year, and it is proper to define the privileges of the day.

Guests on their entrance to the hall are expected to remove overcoats, hats and gloves, so that they can enter the drawing room free to receive and offer salutations.

The reception-room would be warm and beautiful for the festive season. There are many forms in which refreshments may be presented with but little danger for even the weakest, and the palate is not the chief means for social delight. The veriest anchorite would prescribe refreshments for callers

Triple-click to select an entire paragraph

The genial custom of making New Year's calls has some privileges "more honored in the breach than in the observance," but there are few persons in society who would wish to abolish the time-honored license of that festive season, however strenuously they may counsel wise reforms.

The formalities enforced in polite circles at other seasons are relaxed with the coming of the New Year, and it is proper to define the privileges of the day.

Guests on their entrance to the hall are expected to remove overcoats, hats and gloves, so that they can enter the drawing room free to receive and offer salutations.

The reception-room would be warm and beautiful for the festive season. There are many forms in which refreshments may be presented with but little danger for even the weakest, and the palate is not the chief means for social delight. The veriest anchorite would prescribe refreshments for callers

Choose "Select all" from the Edit menu to select the entire story

The genial custom of making New Year's calls has some privileges "more honored in there breach than in the observance," but there are few persons in society who would wish to abolish the t time-honored license of that festive season, however strenuously they may counsel wise reforms .

The formalities enforced in polite circles at other seasons are relaxed with the coming of tf the New Year, and it is proper to define the privileges of the day

Guests on their entrance to the hall are expected to remove overcoats, hats and gloves, soo that they can enter the drawing room free to receive and offer salutations

The reception-room would be warm and beautiful for the festive season. There are many forms in which refreshments may be presented with but little danger for even the weakest, and the palate is not the chief means for social delight. The veriest anchorite would prescribe refreshments for callers

Using the text tool, play around with selecting different ranges of text:

- Double-click to select a word.

- Triple-click to select an entire paragraph.

- Using the text tool, choose "Select all" from the Edit menu to select all the text in a story.

- To deselect text, simply click anywhere outside the selected area.

When you click an insertion point using the *text tool* and then choose "Select all," PageMaker selects all the text in a story, even the parts that are on other pages. If you were to choose "Select all" with the *pointer tool* selected, PageMaker would select all the text as well as any graphic elements on the visible pages and the pasteboard.

For information on what formatting is retained when you place a story in PageMaker, refer to the article "Importing and exporting text and graphics files" in the *Aldus PageMaker 4.0 Reference Manual*.

After selecting text, you can format it directly by choosing "Font," "Size," or "Paragraph…," from the Type menu, or you can apply styles to the text. (Styles store a collection of formatting specifications that change the appearance of text, not its content. There is more about this in Lesson 4 and in the article "Formatting text with styles and style sheets" in the *Aldus PageMaker 4.0 Reference Manual*.)

Changing font size

Experiment with the way the Type menu works by changing a portion of text to 18-point Helvetica.

1. **Using the text tool, select a sentence.**

2. **Choose "Helvetica" from "Font" on the Type menu.**
   Depending on the defaults set on your computer, Helvetica may already be checked.

3. **Choose "18" from "Size" on the Type menu.**
   PageMaker measures text size in points, a system for precisely specifying the size of type. (To give you an idea of how precise, 1 point = 1/72nd of an inch, so 18 points = 1/4 of an inch.)

4. **Return the font size to 12 points.**

1 Using the text tool, select a sentence.

2 Choose "Helvetica."

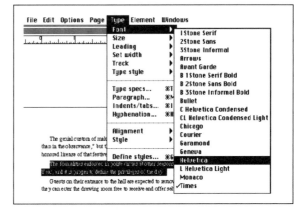

3 Choose 18 points.

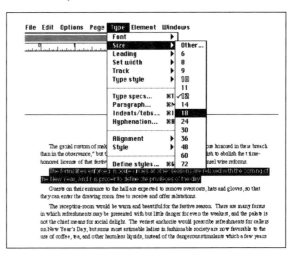

Type size is larger than the rest of text

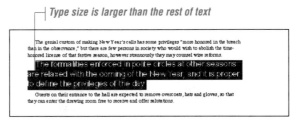

4 Return the font size to 12 points.

Experimenting with text blocks

When you placed "Practice text" on the page, you placed what PageMaker considers to be a story; in this example the story consists of one text block. In the following steps you'll identify a text block and experiment with one of PageMaker's strongest features: the elasticity of its text blocks. You can move them, break them apart, and change their shapes as the page layout and graphic images in your publication dictate, while keeping the flow of the story from block to block intact.

For more information on text blocks, refer to the article "Working with text blocks" in the *Aldus PageMaker 4.0 Reference Manual.* If you want to experiment further with text blocks, try the lesson "Unraveling threaded text" later in this tutorial.

On your own
Changing type style and alignment

Experiment with "Type style" (italic, bold, underline, and so on) and "Alignment" (centered, justified, etc.) on the Type menu. Remember: Use the text tool to select the text you want to change before making a choice from the menu. Watch how the text changes with each choice. Take a few minutes to try out other commands on the Type menu, too.

The genial custom of making New Year's calls has some privileges "more honored in the breach than in the observance," but there are few persons in	The genial custom of making New Year's calls has some privileges "more honored in the breach than in the observance," but there are few persons in	**New Year's Calls** The genial custom of making New Year's calls has some privileges "more honored in the breach than in the observance," but there are few persons in.
Italicized paragraph	*Justified paragraph (text is even on both sides)*	*Centered heading*

Identifying a text block

To identify a text block, select the pointer tool from the toolbox and click in the block. The block is then bounded at top and bottom by a windowshade with loops, called windowshade handles. (Don't confuse the loop with the square handles at the four corners of the text block.)

The windowshade defines the boundary of the text block.

- An empty windowshade handle at the top of a block indicates the beginning of the story; at the end of a block it tells you the whole story has been placed.

- A "+" in a windowshade handle between text blocks indicates there is text from the same story before or after that text block.

- A "▼" in a windowshade handle indicates there is more text to place.

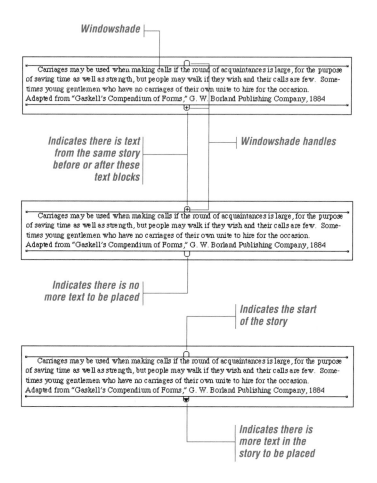

Windowshade

Carriages may be used when making calls if the round of acquaintances is large, for the purpose of saving time as well as strength, but people may walk if they wish and their calls are few. Sometimes young gentlemen who have no carriages of their own unite to hire for the occasion. Adapted from "Gaskell's Compendium of Forms," G. W. Borland Publishing Company, 1884

Indicates there is text from the same story before or after these text blocks

Windowshade handles

Carriages may be used when making calls if the round of acquaintances is large, for the purpose of saving time as well as strength, but people may walk if they wish and their calls are few. Sometimes young gentlemen who have no carriages of their own unite to hire for the occasion. Adapted from "Gaskell's Compendium of Forms," G. W. Borland Publishing Company, 1884

Indicates there is no more text to be placed

Indicates the start of the story

Carriages may be used when making calls if the round of acquaintances is large, for the purpose of saving time as well as strength, but people may walk if they wish and their calls are few. Sometimes young gentlemen who have no carriages of their own unite to hire for the occasion. Adapted from "Gaskell's Compendium of Forms," G. W. Borland Publishing Company, 1884

Indicates there is more text in the story to be placed

1. **Select the pointer tool and click in the text to select the block.**
   In this example there is only one text block.

2. **Drag the bottom windowshade handle up.**
   Point to the handle and, holding down the mouse button, drag up. The block shrinks and a "▼" appears in the bottom windowshade handle indicating there is more text to be placed. This is called rolling up the windowshade.

◆ Did you roll the windowshade handle up all the way so no text is visible? Go ahead with Steps 3 and 4. Then try Steps 1 through 4 again.

   If your windowshade handles disappeared before you could click, choose "Select all" from the Edit menu to make them reappear.

3. **Click in the windowshade handle with a ▼ and release quickly.**
   The loaded text icon appears.

4. **Now click anywhere on the page below the top text block.**
   The text will flow into the space. Now you've created two text blocks. If the windowshade handle of the second text block has a "▼", go to Step 5. Otherwise, you have placed all the text and can skip that step.

① *Using the pointer tool, select the text block.*

② *Drag the bottom windowshade handle up.*

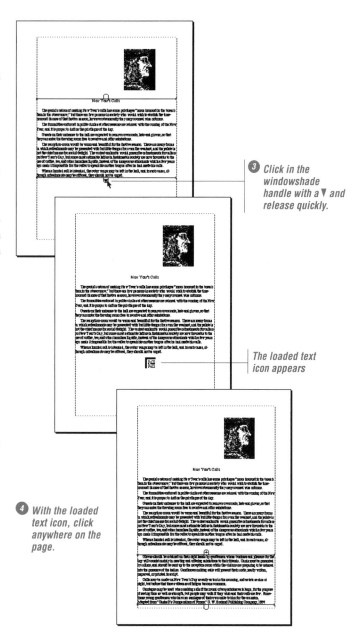

③ *Click in the windowshade handle with a ▼ and release quickly.*

The loaded text icon appears

④ *With the loaded text icon, click anywhere on the page.*

5. **Optional: Drag down the bottom window-shade handle of the second text block.**

   The block expands. When the handle is empty you know there is no more text to place.

◆ If you get the loaded text icon when you don't want it, click on the pointer tool in the toolbox. The loaded text icon will go away.

⑤ *Drag the bottom windowshade handle down.*

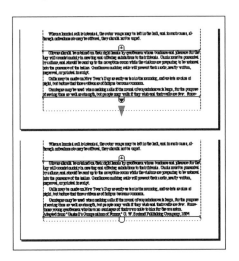

Putting text blocks together

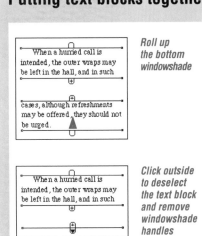

Roll up the bottom windowshade

Click outside to deselect the text block and remove windowshade handles

Now all the text is in one block

If you break a block of text into two or more blocks, it's easy to put the blocks together again. Start with the last text block and drag the bottom handle up past the top handle until the text disappears. Then click outside the block to deselect it.

Roll up the windowshades for all text blocks except the first text block. This does not delete the text in the blocks; it simply pushes the text up into the windowshade of the text block above. The first text block will now have a "▼" in the bottom windowshade handle. Select the first text block and drag the handle down. Text will reappear.

◆ If you accidentally roll up the last windowshade handle, too, and click so it disappears, you can make it visible again by choosing "Select all" from the Edit menu.

If you want to experiment further with combining text blocks, try the lesson "Unraveling threaded text" later in this tutorial or refer to the technique "Combining text blocks" in the *Aldus PageMaker 4.0 Reference Manual.*

Changing the size of a text block

You can resize a text block to fit into any space. You might find this easiest to do from the "Fit in window" display size.

1. Using the pointer, select the bottom text block.

2. Press and hold down the mouse button on a square handle at any windowshade corner until you see a two-directional arrow.

The square handles indicate the text block is selected. They disappear when you see the two-directional arrow.

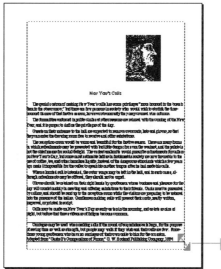

➊ *Using the pointer, select the bottom text block.*

➋ *Press and hold down the mouse button until you see a two-directional arrow.*

Two-directional arrow

3. Without letting go, drag to resize the text block.

Notice that when the block shrinks, the empty handle changes to a "▼", indicating there is more text to place.

◆ To return the text block to its original size repeat Steps 2 and 3.

◆ If you make the text block disappear, simply pull down the bottom windowshade handle to make the text visible again.

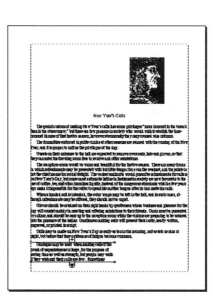

➌ *Without letting go, drag to resize the text block.*

Moving a text block

You can move blocks of text, too, just as you moved the graphic.

1. Using the pointer, select the text block you want to move.

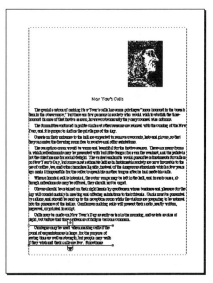

❶ *Select the text block you want to move.*

2. Hold down the mouse button anywhere inside the text block until you see a four-headed arrow. Without letting go, drag the block to the new spot.

◆ If the image of Aldus Manutius moves along with the text, it's because it is selected, too; perhaps you chose "Select all" from the Edit menu using the pointer tool. Click outside the page, then repeat Steps 1 and 2 again.

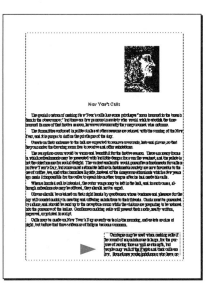

❷ *Drag the block to the new spot.*

Saving your work

When you work on a computer, generally your work is stored in a part of the computer's memory that is not a permanent storage place; when you turn off your computer, that information will be erased from memory. To avoid losing your work, you should save it frequently on the hard disk, a more permanent storage device in your computer. Your disk, like a cassette tape, is reusable and you can copy the information in memory onto the disk.

We strongly recommend saving to the hard disk at least every 15 minutes. That way, if your computer gets switched off or there's a power failure, you'll never lose more than 15 minutes' work.

To get in the habit now, follow the steps on the next page to save the publication you've been working on. Saving files in PageMaker is the same as saving files in other Macintosh applications: You choose "Save..." from the File menu and give the file a name.

Automatic saving

PageMaker automatically saves your work each time you do certain tasks, such as copying, printing, clicking a page icon (even the icon of the page you're on), inserting or removing a page, or changing the page setup. PageMaker uses these mini-saves to recover from a malfunction of your computer or a loss of power—a kind of insurance that PageMaker offers when you need it. The next time you open the publication after the malfunction, PageMaker opens the mini-saved version instead of the version you last saved, which is probably older. For example, if you had inserted a new page and placed some text on the page and there were a power outage, PageMaker would save the new page but not the text placed on it. However, if you had also turned to another page after placing the text, it too would be saved.

You don't want to rely on PageMaker to do your saving for you. When you save your publication, you are in the driver's seat, controlling precisely what is saved and when. When you use "Save" or "Save as...," PageMaker makes the saved version and the mini-saved version the same.

For more information on saving, refer to the "Save" and "Revert" command descriptions in the *Aldus PageMaker 4.0 Reference Manual*.

1. **Choose "Save" from the File menu.**

2. **In the edit box, type the name you want for the publication and click "OK."**

The next time you save, PageMaker will not ask you to name your file. It will assume you want to save it with the same name unless you use "Save as…" from the File menu.

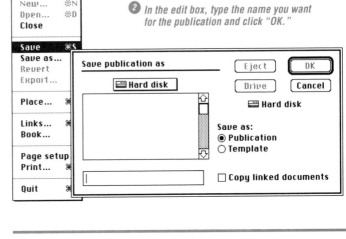

1 *Choose "Save" from the File menu.*

2 *In the edit box, type the name you want for the publication and click "OK."*

What next?

If you are new to desktop publishing and PageMaker and you are comfortable with this step-by-step approach to learning the program, you can go on to the next lesson, the first of four that take you through the design and layout of a newsletter. If you learn best by experimentation, you may be ready to try using PageMaker to produce a publication of your own. You can always come back to the tutorial to pick up techniques you need help with.

If you are an experienced user of other desktop publishing programs, but new to PageMaker, you may want to skim through the newsletter project, practicing the features that are new to you. You might also want to try your hand at the "Practice topics," as these give you a glimpse at how PageMaker handles indents, tabs, and the flow of text between text blocks.

1. **Choose "Close" from the File menu.**
   This closes this publication and returns you to the PageMaker desktop.

2. **Choose "Quit" from the File menu to exit PageMaker.**
   This shuts down PageMaker and returns you to the Macintosh desktop.

1 *Choose "Close" from the File menu.*

2 *Choose "Quit" from the File menu to exit PageMaker.*

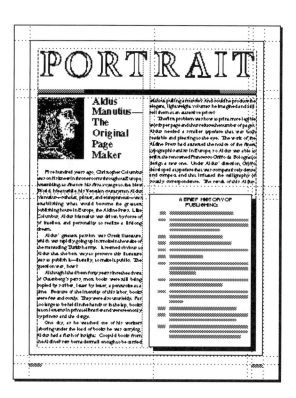

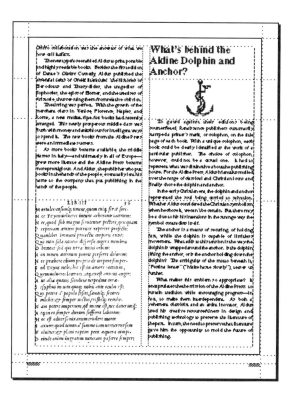

Producing a newsletter: Lessons 1 through 4

In these four lessons, you'll learn how to use PageMaker 4.0 by creating a two-page newsletter. You'll find the lessons easiest to do if you've worked through "Getting down to basics," the introductory lesson. When you have finished, you will have a two-page newsletter that looks like the example above.

Lesson 1: Setting up the newsletter

The finished master page will look like this

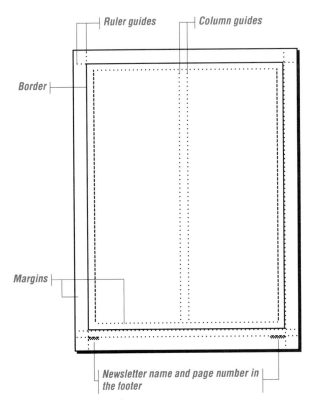

Ruler guides   Column guides

Border

Margins

Newsletter name and page number in the footer

Lesson 1 focuses on setting up the master page for the two-page newsletter you'll complete in Lessons 2 through 4. The master page is the foundation for any publication you create in PageMaker; every element you want to repeat on each page of a publication goes on the master page. This ensures a consistent look for the entire publication and is a great time-saver because you create these elements only once rather than copying them onto each page.

In this lesson you'll set margins and two columns for the text. Then you'll create a border that surrounds each page and add a footer with the newsletter name and the page number. You'll learn how to:

- Set margins

- Create columns

- Position ruler guides

- Draw a border

- Type and position text on a page

- Number pages

What's in this lesson

Starting a new publication

As in "Getting down to basics" and with all Macintosh applications, you start a new publication using the "New…" command.

1. **Optional: Open the folder containing PageMaker 4.0 and double-click the PageMaker 4.0 icon.**
   If you're already in PageMaker, ignore this step.

2. **Choose the "New…" command from the File menu.**

3. **Make sure the options in the "Page setup" dialog box are set as shown here.**
   When you uncheck "Double-sided," PageMaker assumes you will be printing or photocopying on one side of the paper.

4. **Click "OK."**
   PageMaker displays the pasteboard with a letter-size vertical page.

◆ If you have a master page icon that shows two pages, you forgot to uncheck the "Double-sided" option in the "Page setup" dialog box. Choose "Page setup" from the File menu and make the change.

➊ *Open PageMaker 4.0.*

➋ *Choose the "New…" command from the File menu.*

➌ *Make sure the options in the "Page setup" dialog box are set as shown here.*

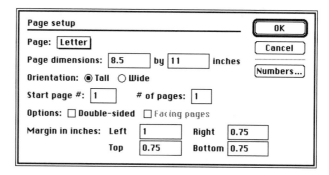

➍ *Click "OK."*

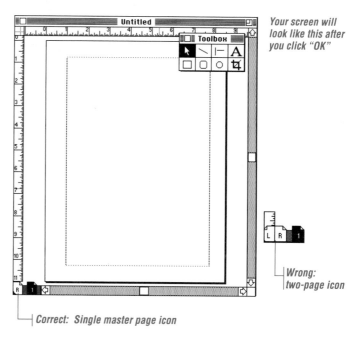

Your screen will look like this after you click "OK"

Wrong: two-page icon

Correct: Single master page icon

Setting up the newsletter

Before you proceed, make sure the settings for your newsletter are the same as those required for working through this tutorial. PageMaker's preset options (or defaults) are what PageMaker uses unless you specify otherwise.

You'll change the publication defaults for both the measurement system and the way certain elements are displayed in PageMaker. Setting these preferences and options is somewhat like an orchestra tuning up before a performance so everyone is in tune: It increases the chance that you'll be able to reproduce on the screen what you see in this book.

1. Choose "Preferences..." from the Edit menu.

2. Make sure the options in the "Preferences" dialog box are set as shown here and click "OK."
You'll find some of these settings are already set correctly. To type in the dialog box, tab until you select the setting and then type.

3. Check your screen for the objects shown: two rulers, the toolbox, and scroll bars.
If you don't see the ruler, choose "Rulers" from the Options menu. If you don't see either the toolbox or the scroll bars, choose the commands from the Windows menu.

1 *Choose "Preferences..." from the Edit menu.*

2 *Enter these options:*

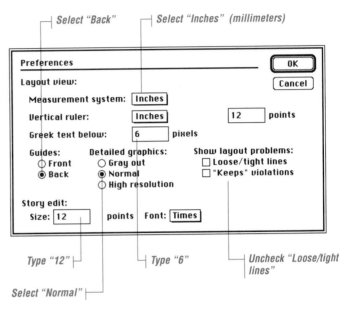

3 *Check your screen for two rulers, the toolbox, and scroll bars.*

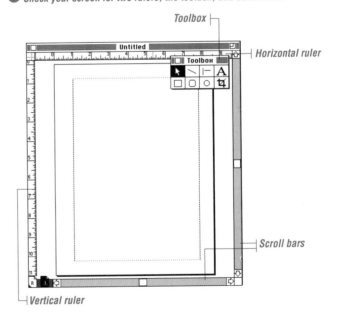

Setting margins

1. Choose "Page setup..." from the File menu.

The dialog box is similar to the one that PageMaker displays when you open a publication. You can set the margins (or any of the options in this dialog box) when you open a new file, or later, as you are doing now.

2. Change the preset margins by tabbing to select each setting. Type the new settings as shown here and click "OK."

When you click "OK," the page may look essentially the same, but PageMaker has already set the new margins.

❶ *Choose "Page setup..." from the File menu.*

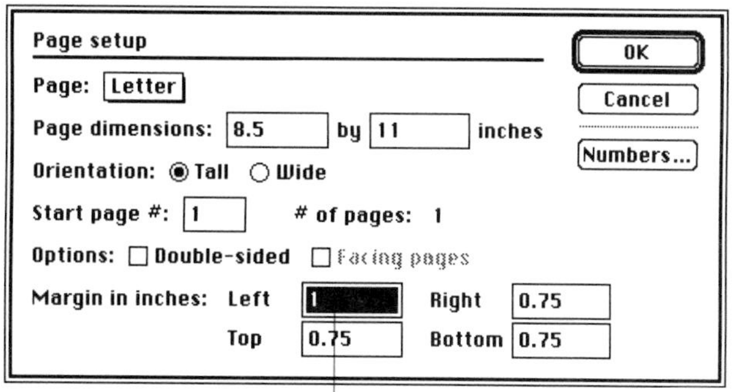

Page setup

Page: Letter

Page dimensions: 8.5 by 11 inches

Orientation: ● Tall ○ Wide

Start page #: 1   # of pages: 1

Options: ☐ Double-sided ☐ Facing pages

Margin in inches: Left 1 Right 0.75
Top 0.75 Bottom 0.75

OK Cancel Numbers...

❷ *Change the left margin to 0.75 (20mm) and change the bottom margin to 1" (30mm).*

More about defaults

You can set defaults (preset options) that affect many parts of your publication: a default font, a default measurement system, a default line weight, and so on. After you specify a default font, for example, any text you type in PageMaker will then match those specifications. You can set defaults for every publication you open in PageMaker (program defaults) or only for the current publication (publication defaults).

You change program defaults after you open PageMaker. Do this when there is no publication open and you have chosen the pointer. Then you'll be able to change the program default for any menu command that is not dimmed. The new values will apply to all new publications you open but will not affect those you've already created.

You change publication defaults at any time after a publication is open (as you're doing for this newsletter). Use the pointer and make sure no elements are selected before you set the defaults. Publication defaults do not affect any other existing publication.

Designing the master page

The master page is the cornerstone in the production of any publication you create in PageMaker. It helps you set a consistent look for each page and saves you time. Think of a master page as a blueprint for every page in your publication: Everything you put on it will appear on every page of your publication. The master page is indicated by an icon, which you click to turn to the master page itself.

In the following steps you'll create the elements of the master page for the tutorial newsletter: two columns for text, a border for the page, and a footer with the newsletter name and page number.

• Click the master page icon.

• **Click the master page icon to turn to the master page.**

Note: Make sure the master page icon is highlighted; if you set the master page elements on page 1 rather than on the master page, you may have a great deal of work to undo later.

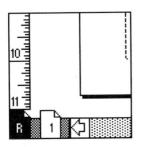

The master page icon is highlighted when you've turned to the master page

◆ If your master page icon has two pages, you forgot to uncheck the "Double-sided" option in the "Page setup" dialog box. Choose "Page setup..." from the File menu and make the change.

Creating columns

Column guides control the alignment of text and graphics within the publication. To ensure that the columns are exactly the same on both pages, you create them on the master page using the "Column guides…" command. For this newsletter, you'll create two columns.

1. **Choose "Column guides…" from the Options menu.**

2. **Type 2 for "Number of columns." Press Tab and type .25 (10mm) for "Space between columns," then click "OK."** Two columns appear on your page.

◆ If you make a mistake in setting up columns—for example, you specify more than two columns or too much space between the columns—it's easy to correct. Choose "Column guides…" from the Options menu again and make the changes you want.

❶ Choose "Column guides…" from the Options menu.

❷ Enter these values:

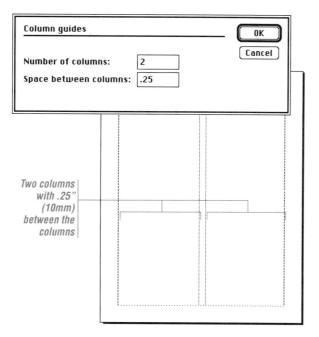

Two columns with .25" (10mm) between the columns

The master page will look like this after you click "OK."

Positioning ruler guides

Ruler guides are nonprinting extensions of the tick marks on the rulers. They help you position design elements, such as a page number, the top of a picture frame, or the border on the page. Because ruler guides are used for alignment purposes only, they do not print.

As you may already have noticed, whenever you move the pointer on the page, PageMaker tracks the position of the pointer with a dotted line in both horizontal and vertical rulers. This tracking helps you to position the ruler guides.

On the master page, you'll position four ruler guides for the border that will lie just outside the margins. Look at page 56 to see how the ruler guides will look when you've finished.

For more information on positioning ruler guides, refer to the technique "Using the zero point to create a layout grid" in the *Aldus PageMaker 4.0 Reference Manual*.

1. Hold down the Command + Option + Shift keys and click in the top-left corner of the page.

This does two things. It zooms you to the top of the page and it changes the page display size of your publication to "200% size," which is large enough to ensure precision when you place the ruler guides.

◆ If your screen does not look like this, it may be that you were not in "Fit in window" size before you did Step 1. To get to "200% size," choose "Fit in window" from the Page menu and repeat Step 1.

❶ *Hold down the Command + Option + Shift keys and click.*

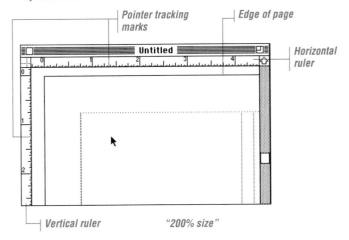

Pointer tracking marks

Edge of page

Horizontal ruler

Vertical ruler

"200% size"

2. Choose "Snap to rulers" from the Options menu.

When you turn on "Snap to rulers," the ruler exerts a magnetic pull on the pointer as it comes close to the tick mark on the ruler. This ensures exact placement of the ruler guides.

3. Place the pointer on the horizontal ruler and, holding down the mouse button, drag a ruler guide down to the 1/2-inch (1.5cm) mark on the vertical ruler.

The pointer changes to a two-headed arrow; the dotted line (a light blue line on color monitors) is the ruler guide.

In the next steps you'll position three more ruler guides around each side of the page, 1/4-inch (50mm) outside each margin.

◆ If the ruler guide disappears, it's because you let go of it before it reached the page; repeat Step 3.

◆ If you want to remove a ruler guide, simply drag it off the page. If the ruler guide doesn't move, choose "Lock guides" on the Options menu to turn off (uncheck) the command. The guides are locked when the command has a check mark beside it.

4. Point inside the vertical ruler. Drag the ruler guide to the 1/2-inch (1.5cm) mark on the horizontal ruler.

This positions the left ruler guide for the left border.

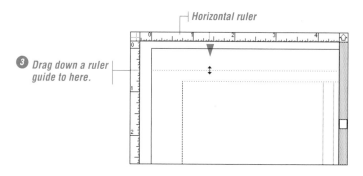

❷ *Choose "Snap to rulers" from the Options menu.*

❸ *Drag down a ruler guide to here.*

Horizontal ruler

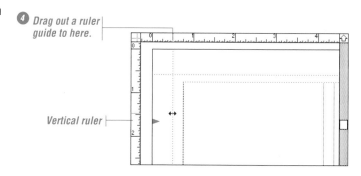

❹ *Drag out a ruler guide to here.*

Vertical ruler

5. From "Fit in window" page display size, zoom to the lower-right corner of the page.

◆ Using a "big picture" display size such as "Fit in window" makes it easiest to move quickly to the bottom of a page. If you've forgotten how to zoom between page display sizes, you'll find a reminder on page 40 in "Getting down to basics."

6. Drag out a ruler guide to 8" (19.5cm) on the horizontal ruler. Drag a ruler guide to 10-1/4" (20.5cm) on the vertical ruler.

◆ If you can't place the ruler guides as described, perhaps you zoomed to the lower-left corner of the page. Start again with Step 5.

7. Choose "Lock guides" from the Options menu.
This option locks the ruler guides in place so you can't accidentally reposition them. The guides are locked when the command has a check mark beside it.

8. Save your work.
Save your work with the name "Lesson 1" and mark your place in the manual. That way, if you take a break before you finish, you can easily pick up where you left off and the file will contain all your work to this point.

⑤ *From "Fit in window" page display size, zoom to lower-right corner of page.*

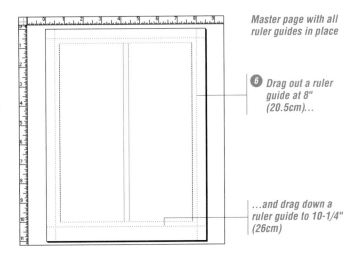

Master page with all ruler guides in place

⑥ *Drag out a ruler guide at 8" (20.5cm)...*

...and drag down a ruler guide to 10-1/4" (26cm)

⑦ *Choose "Lock guides" from the Options menu.*

⑧ *Save your work.*

Drawing the border

Now that you've positioned the ruler guides, it's a simple matter to draw a border. You'll trace the border using the square-corner tool from the toolbox.

1. **Make sure "Snap to guides" from the Options menu is checked.**
   With this command checked, the box you draw will align precisely with the ruler guides, just as the ruler guides aligned with the ruler tick marks.

❶ Check "Snap to guides" from the Options menu.

PageMaker's nonprinting guides

You've now been introduced to all three of PageMaker's nonprinting guides. You see them on the screen and use them in your work, but they don't print. Using guides, rulers, and the "Snap to rulers" and "Snap to guides" commands allows you to position elements on the page with remarkable accuracy: up to 1/2880th (0.00882mm) of an inch, which is higher than a Linotronic 300, one of today's highest-resolution printers, can reproduce.

- Margin guides mark the page margins. They're defined in the "Page setup" dialog box.

- Column guides mark the left and right edges of the columns you create and are used to align text and graphics vertically. PageMaker's default is one column. When you want to specify more than one column, use the "Column guides..." command on the Options menu.

- Ruler guides are extensions of the tick marks on the rulers; you drag ruler guides into the publication from the rulers. Unlike margin and column guides, you'll add and remove ruler guides as you work. On the master page, position ruler guides you want repeated throughout the publication. On individual pages, you can use ruler guides to align design elements, such as rules, the top of a picture frame, or the baseline of a heading.

2. Select the square-corner tool from the toolbox.

When you select the square-corner tool and move it to the page, it takes the shape of a crossbar.

3. In "Fit in window" page display size, point where the ruler guides intersect in the upper-left corner of the newsletter and drag down to the lower-right corner, where the guides intersect again.

If the box doesn't align exactly with the ruler guides, choose the pointer. Point to a corner of the box and, holding down the mouse button, drag to resize the box.

(If you try to draw the border using the square-corner tool again, you'll just draw another box. If you do create another box, delete it by selecting it with the pointer tool and pressing the Delete key.)

◆ If you need a reminder on how to switch page display sizes, turn to page 40 in "Getting down to basics."

◆ If you're still having trouble getting the borders exactly on top of the ruler guides, you may have forgotten to choose "Snap to guides" from the Options menu. Do that and try Step 3 again.

◆ If the border line is too thick, choose "1 pt" from "Line" on the Element menu and repeat Step 3 again.

◆ If the borders seem to disappear, it's because you haven't selected "Back" for "Guides" in the "Preferences" dialog box. Return to page 58, and repeat Steps 1 and 2.

② *Select the square-corner tool.*

③ *Start dragging here and...*

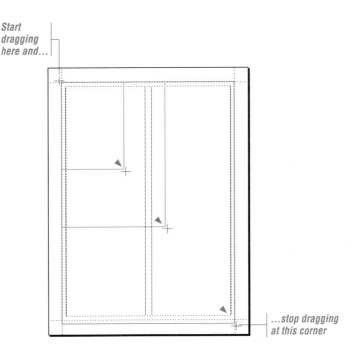

...stop dragging at this corner

The master page now has a border around the margins

Creating a text footer

A footer is text that appears at the bottom
of every page of a publication. Typically,
a two-page newsletter would not need a
footer. However, because most newsletters are longer than two pages, we'll
show you how to create two footers: one
with the name of the newsletter, the other
with the page number.

First you'll position a ruler guide to
align the top of the footer; then you'll
specify the font and type size for the
footer. Last, you'll type the footer and
place it on the page.

**1. Using the pointer tool, zoom to the lower-
left of the page at "200% size."**

◆ If the page 1 icon is highlighted you've
been working on page 1, not the master
page. *Stop now!* Click the master page
icon to turn to the master page. If the
master page is blank, start again.

To start over, return to page 1.
Using the pointer, choose "Select all"
from the Edit menu and press Delete.
Click the master page icon once more,
and go back to page 60 to follow the
steps to set up the master page.

**2. Drag a ruler guide down to the 10-1/2"
(21cm) mark on the vertical ruler.**
You'll use this ruler guide to line up the
top of the footer.

◆ If you let go of the ruler guide too
soon, choose "Lock guides" from the
Options menu to turn off the command
before trying to reposition the ruler
guide.

❶ Zoom in.

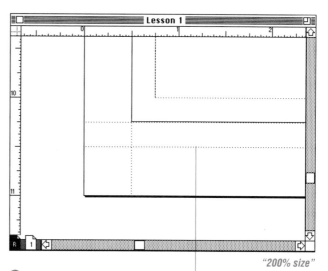

"200% size"

*❷ Drag a ruler guide to 10-1/2"
(21cm) on the vertical ruler.*

3. **Choose "Type specs..." from the Type menu.**

   When you use the pointer tool here, you determine the text style for the entire publication; everything you type in this newsletter from now on will appear in the font you choose here. (If you use the text tool and click in the text, the choices you make from the menu apply only to the text you are about to type.) And, of course, you can always override these defaults by selecting the text using the text tool and changing it.

4. **Choose "Times" from "Font" in the "Type specifications" dialog box.**

   Times is the default font and may already be selected.

5. **Choose "10" (points) from "Size" in the "Type specifications" dialog box, then click "OK."**

   Steps 4 and 5 determined the font and size of the newsletter name in the footer. Because you made these font and size selections with no text selected, whatever you type from now on will display as 10-point Times.

6. **Select the text tool and position the crossbar of the I-beam at the intersection of the horizontal ruler guide and the left border guide.**

   The text tool changes to an I-beam when you move it to the page.

③ *Choose "Type specs..." from the Type menu.*

④ *Choose "Times" for "Font."*

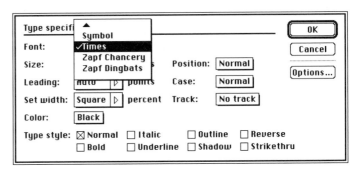

⑤ *Choose "10" for "Size"*

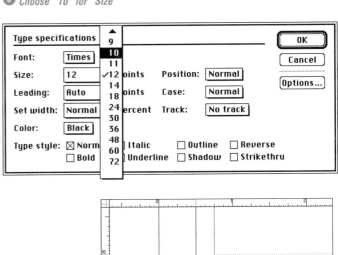

⑥ *Position the I-beam crossbar here.*

7. Drag the I-beam diagonally down to the right just enough to draw a small box.

As you drag, you see the small box. When you finish dragging and release the mouse button, the box disappears and the insertion point appears at the border. (The insertion point is a tiny flashing vertical line, PageMaker's way of indicating it's ready for you to type.)

You create the box to control the width of the text block. Without the box, the text block would be the width of the page, a size that is cumbersome for this footer.

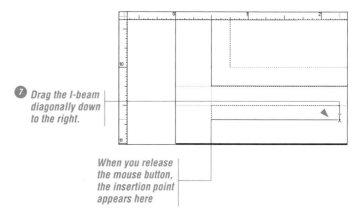

❼ Drag the I-beam diagonally down to the right.

When you release the mouse button, the insertion point appears here

Elements of type

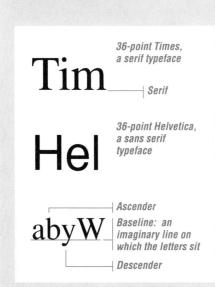

36-point Times, a serif typeface

Serif

36-point Helvetica, a sans serif typeface

Ascender

Baseline: an imaginary line on which the letters sit

Descender

How appealing your publication looks and how easy it is to read depend in part on the typeface, or font, you use. We chose Times because we felt that a serif typeface worked best with the content of this newsletter. (Serifs are the tiny appendages projecting from a letter.) Although there are literally thousands of typefaces, they can be grouped into two basic styles: serif and sans serif (meaning, literally, without serifs).

PageMaker and many desktop publishing programs use points to measure type. In desktop publishing, a point is equal to exactly 1/72nd of an inch. (This is different from the point used in traditional publishing in the United States and Great Britain, which is very slightly smaller than 1/72nd of an inch.) Type style refers to the weight or slant of a letter—whether it is bold or italic—and whether it has such features as a shadow or an outline.

8. Type *Portrait*, the name of the newsletter.

9. Using the pointer, click inside the text block to check the position of the footer. Make sure the top windowshade handle snaps to the horizontal guide, and that the left edge of the text block lines up with the vertical ruler guide. Drag the block as necessary to make the alignment precise. (To deselect the text block, click anywhere outside the text block.)

◆ If the word "Portrait" doesn't fit in the box you've drawn, you can resize the text block. Using the pointer, click anywhere in the word "Portrait" to select it. Point to a right handle and drag to expand the box. You should see the word clearly now. If not, try again.

8️⃣ *Type Portrait.*

9️⃣ *Check the position of the text block.*

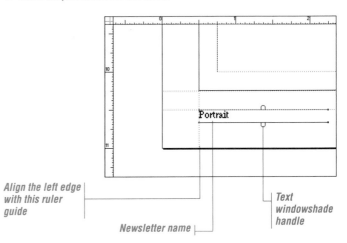

Align the left edge with this ruler guide

Newsletter name

Text windowshade handle

Setting the default font

When you type, PageMaker uses the publication default font and point size to format the text. When you choose a font and point size without any text selected or the insertion point active, you reset the publication defaults (as you have just done in this lesson). When you're about to create several text blocks using a font that's different from the publication default, be sure to select the font and point size you want *before* you select the text tool and click the insertion point. Otherwise, you'll have to go back and select each text block and reformat it with the font and size you want.

Adding a page number

Next you'll create another footer—a page number—and align it on the lower right of the page. You've already placed the bottom ruler guide, so all you have to do is insert the page number, align it on the right, and position it on the page.

1. **Zoom to the lower-right edge of the page.**

◆ Does the footer become a gray box when you go to "Fit in window" size? This is perfectly normal and happens whenever the type size is too small for PageMaker to show in that page display size.

2. **Using the text tool, position the crossbar of the I-beam at the intersection of the horizontal ruler and the right border guide.**

3. **Drag the I-beam diagonally down to the left to draw a small box.**
   This creates a space in which you type the page-number marker.

4. **Type** *Page* **and press the spacebar to insert a space.**

5. **Press Command + Option + P to insert the page-number character.**
   This inserts a special character that tells PageMaker to advance the page number on each page. It appears as "RM" (right master page) or "LM" (left master page), depending on which master page you are on. In the newsletter, the page number will appear as the correct number.
       Next, you'll align the page number with the right border guide.

1 Zoom to the lower-right edge of the page.

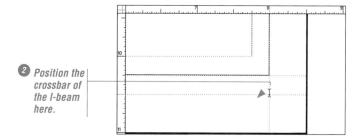

2 Position the crossbar of the I-beam here.

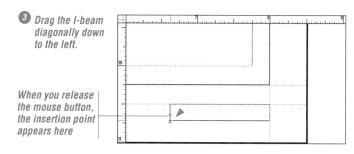

3 Drag the I-beam diagonally down to the left.

When you release the mouse button, the insertion point appears here

4 Type Page*.*

5 Press Option + Command + P to insert the page number.

Page RM

◆ If you can't see the right margin now, you made the box too big. To make the box smaller, use the pointer to click the page number and display the text block handles. Drag a corner handle to shrink the box.

6. Choose "Align right" from "Alignment" on the Type menu.

The page number pops over to the right border guide.

◆ If "Page RM" did not move on your screen, perhaps the insertion point was no longer on the words "Page RM." Using the text tool, click an insertion point in "Page RM" and try Step 6 again.

7. Save your work.

Press Command + S to save your work quickly and easily.

Finishing up the master page

It's good practice when you think you've finished the master page to step back and check to see if it meets your requirements. Zoom to the "Fit in window" page display size to make sure your master page looks like this one. If it doesn't, make a note of the elements that differ and return to the sections in this lesson that show you how to create them. You'll find the next lesson easier if you make the changes now.

6 Choose "Align right."

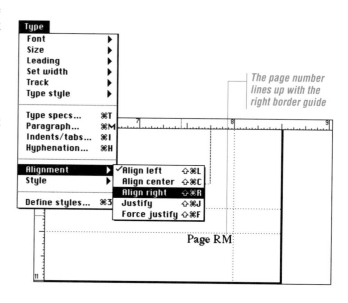

The page number lines up with the right border guide

7 Save your work.

Your master page should look like this

Column guides

Border

Newsletter title footer

Page number aligned right

Page numbering in PageMaker

You can change the format of page numbers. For example, to number a preface to a book with lowercase Roman numerals, choose "Page setup…" from the File menu and click the "Numbers" button. Then select from one of five number formats in the "Page numbering" dialog box.

Typically, when you are working on a large project, you'll want to break it up into several smaller publications to make the files easier to manage. To ensure that pages are numbered consecutively from one publication to the next, type the starting page number for that publication in the "Start page #" option in the "Page setup" dialog box. PageMaker can number pages up to 9999, although any one publication may not exceed 999 pages.

```
Page numbering                              [  OK  ]

Style:   ⦿ Arabic numeral   1, 2, 3, …       [ Cancel ]
         ○ Upper Roman      I, II, III, …
         ○ Lower Roman      i, ii, iii, …
         ○ Upper alphabetic  A, B, C, … AA, BB, CC, …
         ○ Lower alphabetic  a, b, c, … aa, bb, cc, …

TOC and index prefix: [                    ]
```

What next?

This is the end of the first lesson. When you continue with Lesson 2, you'll place the first story on the page along with the masthead (the title of the newsletter) and a drawing of Aldus Manutius, the Venetian scholar and printer who established the Aldine Press, the greatest publishing house of 15th-century Europe.

Lesson 2: Laying out page one

Page 1 will almost be finished at the end of this lesson

Masthead with "Portrait" logotype

ID line

Image of Aldus

Text wrapped around graphic

Lead story

With the master page set up in Lesson 1, you're ready to start the work of laying out the newsletter. In Lesson 2, you'll lay out most of the first page. First you'll create the masthead and place the lead story. Then you'll place the graphic image of Aldus Manutius that starts the column, and wrap the text around it.

In this lesson you'll learn how to:

• Layer text and graphics

• Set tabs

• Wrap text around a graphic

What's in this lesson

Building the newsletter masthead

Now you'll begin laying out the first page of the newsletter with the masthead. This area, usually across the top of a newsletter's first page, consists of the newsletter name and the issue's date and volume. The masthead is designed to catch the reader's attention; for this newsletter, the masthead includes a logotype created in Aldus FreeHand. (The *logotype* is a distinctive typeface and design that identifies the publication.) The identification (or ID) line, which contains the publication date, volume, and number of the newsletter, is a single text block set in reverse type: light text on a dark background.

You'll find the tasks of building the newsletter masthead easiest if you're comfortable switching from one page display size to another, particularly between "Fit in window" and "Actual size." If you need a reminder on how to change display sizes, return to page 40 in "Getting down to basics."

The newsletter masthead

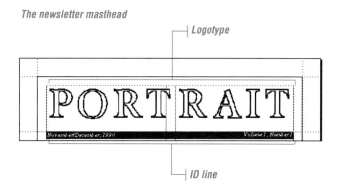

Turning the page

1. **Optional: Open the Tutorial folder and then the Lesson 2 folder. Last, open the "Lesson 1 done" file.**
   If you're beginning with this lesson, open "Lesson 1 done" before proceeding. If you're continuing from Lesson 1, proceed with the next step.

2. **Turn to page 1 by clicking the page icon.**

❶ *Optional: Open the Tutorial folder and then the Lesson 2 folder. Last, open the "Lesson 1 done" file.*

❷ *Click the page icon.*

Note: *Don't forget to turn to page 1 before laying out the first page of your publication.* It's easy to forget, but if you don't turn to page 1, everything will be placed on the master page. All the elements placed on the master page print on all other pages.

Placing the "Portrait" logotype

1. **Choose "Place..." from the File menu. Select "Logotype.eps" in the Lesson 2 list box of the Tutorial folder, and click "OK."**
This list box shows the names of files in the Lesson 2 folder. The "Logotype.eps" file is a graphic image created in Aldus FreeHand. It was saved on the disk in the EPS file format.

   You may find the logotype easiest to place from "Fit in window" page display size.

◆ If this file is not in the Lesson 2 list box, refer to the notes you made on page 33 in "Getting down to basics" for a reminder on where to find tutorial files.

2. **Click to place the logotype somewhere near the top of the page.**
This places the masthead logotype, "Portrait," onto the page; you'll position it more precisely in the next step.

1 *Choose "Place..." from the file menu and select "Logotype.eps."*

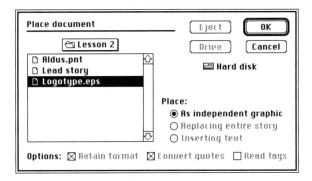

2 *Click the EPS icon to place the logotype.*

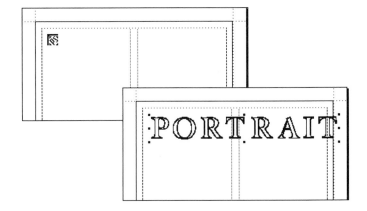

3. **Using the pointer, position the graphic so the top and left edges of the logotype's boundary line up with the top and left margins.**

◆ Did you accidentally distort the shape of the graphic? This happened because you pointed to a square handle when you dragged the graphic. To return the graphic to its original proportions (though not necessarily its original size), first select the graphic using the pointer. Press the Shift key while you drag a square handle to resize.

❸ *Drag the graphic so its top and left edges line up with the page margins.*

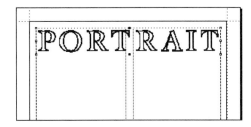

Typing and formatting the ID line

Now you will type and italicize the ID line for the newsletter.

1. **Using the text tool, click anywhere inside the left-hand column.**

❶ *Click inside the left-hand column.*

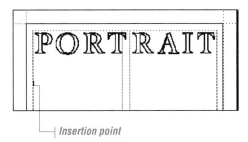

Insertion point

2. **At the insertion point, type** *November/ December 1990,* **then press Tab and type** *Volume 1, Number 1.*
   You will find this easiest to do from a close-up page display size. You insert the tab so that later you can align the volume number at the right margin.

◆ If you're in a close-up view, you'll notice the font is Times. If you're wondering what sort of magic determined the font, remember you set the default font in Lesson 1 as 10-point Times for any text you type in the publication.

❷ *Type the text for the ID line.*

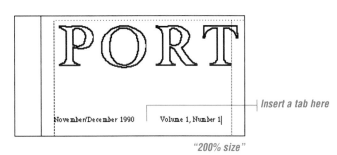

Insert a tab here

November/December 1990   Volume 1, Number 1

"200% size"

3. **Using the text tool, triple-click to select the ID line.**

   Now you are ready to italicize the text. (Make sure you are using the text tool when you triple-click. If you triple-click using the pointer, you will land in the story editor.)

   ◆ If you accidentally get in the story editor, choose "Place" from the File menu to return to layout view.

4. **Choose "Italic" from "Type style" on the Type menu.**

③ *Triple-click to select the ID line.*

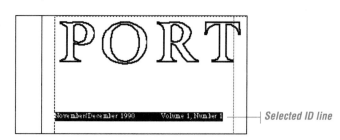

Selected ID line

④ *Choose "Italic."*

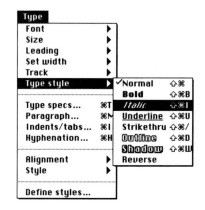

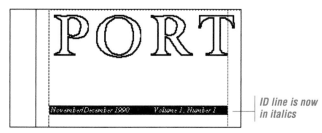

ID line is now in italics

Positioning the ID line

1. Using the pointer, drag a horizontal ruler guide to 2" (8cm) from the top of the page.
You'll use this guide to position the top of the ID line.

◆ If you need to reposition the ruler guide, choose "Lock guides" on the Options menu to turn off (uncheck) the command.

2. Size the text block so it spans the width of the page.
You will find this easiest to do from "Fit in window" display size. Make sure the block extends from margin to margin, not from border to border; the text will remain aligned left until you set a right-aligned tab later.

◆ Remember, to size a text block, first select the text using the pointer. Drag a square handle until the text block is the size you want.

◆ Did your text disappear completely? You may have rolled up the windowshade so the text and the windowshade disappeared. The text is still there even though you can't see it. To restore it, choose "Select all" from the Edit menu. Then drag the bottom windowshade handle down to reveal the text.

3. Position the ID line so the top edge of the windowshade snaps to the 2" (8cm) ruler guide.

❶ *Drag a horizontal ruler guide to 2" (8cm).*

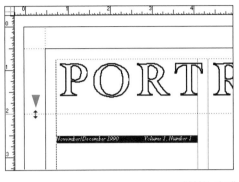

"200% size"

❷ *Size the text block by dragging a corner handle.*

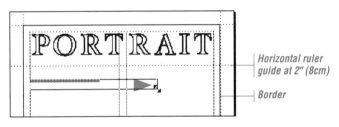

"Fit in window"

Horizontal ruler guide at 2" (8cm)

Border

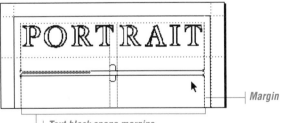

Margin

Text block spans margins

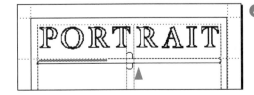

❸ *Drag the ID line up until the top of the windowshade snaps to the ruler guide.*

Moving the volume number to the right

Now you are ready to align the newsletter volume number with the right margin by setting a right tab marker.

If you want to know more about setting and using tabs, see the lesson "Setting indents and tabs" in this tutorial or refer to the "Indents/tabs..." command description in the *Aldus PageMaker 4.0 Reference Manual*.

1. Using the text tool, click an insertion point in the ID line.

2. Change to "Fit in window" page display size if necessary.
You won't be able to see the details of the text, but this display size will make it easiest to set the tab stop.

3. Choose "Indents/tabs..." from the Type menu.

◆ Is the right margin marker in a different location from the one shown here or perhaps not even visible at all? The ruler in the "Indents/tabs..." dialog box changes for different page display sizes so cancel the dialog box and start again at Step 2.

4. Select the right tab marker and click near the right margin marker at about 6.5" (16cm) on the ruler.
You'll move the right tab marker into position in the next step.

1 Click an insertion point in the ID line.

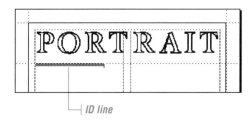

ID line

2 Change to "Fit in window" page display size, if necessary.

3 Choose "Indents/tabs..." from the Type menu.

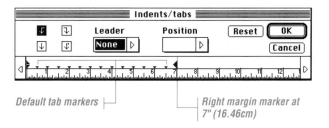

Default tab markers

Right margin marker at 7" (16.46cm)

4 Select the right tab marker and click at about 6.5" (16cm)

Right tab marker

"Position" box displays marker position

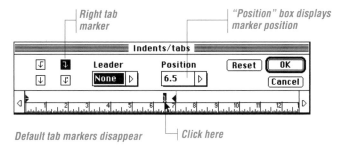

Default tab markers disappear

Click here

**5. Drag the right tab marker until "7"
(16.46cm) appears in the "Position" box.**
The tab marker will be on top of the
right margin marker.

⑤ *Drag the right tab marker to the margin marker.*

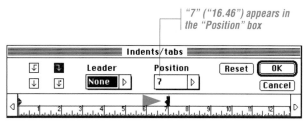

*"7" ("16.46") appears in
the "Position" box*

6. Click "OK."
The right tab marker forces the
volume number to line up at the
right margin.

⑥ *Click "OK."*

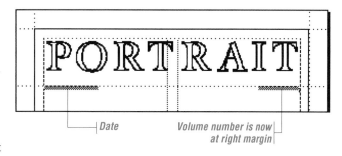

Date | Volume number is now
at right margin

Creating the black ID rule

The last step in creating the masthead
is to make the text white and the rule
black. To do this, you'll draw a 12-point
black line and then send it behind the
white text.

**1. From the "Fit in window" page display
size, use the text tool to select the entire
text block.**

① *Triple-click to select the entire text block.*

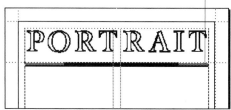

② *Choose "Reverse" from "Type style" on the
Type menu.*

**2. Choose "Reverse" from "Type style"
on the Type menu.**
This reverses the color of the text
from black to white so later it will be
visible on the black line. In "Fit in
window" page display size, nothing
appears to change.

◆ If nothing happened, you may have
selected the "Portrait" logotype
rather than the text block. Start with
Step 1 again.

◆ If the text disappears in a close-up page display, you're looking at white text on a white background. Return to "Fit in window" to see the line as a grey bar.

3. Select the perpendicular-line tool from the toolbox.

When you choose the line tool and move it to the page, it takes the shape of a crossbar.

③ *Select the perpendicular-line tool.*

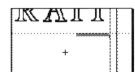

The cursor changes to a crossbar

4. Choose "12 pt" from "Line" on the Element menu.

"12 pt" refers to the thickness of the rule you're about to draw.

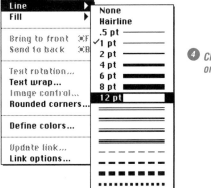

④ *Choose "12 pt" from "Line" on the Element menu.*

5. Using the perpendicular-line tool, drag to draw the rule under the 2" (8cm) ruler guide from the left to the right margin.

Drawing the rule created a second layer. The text seems to disappear in the black rule because the black rule is on top of the text.

◆ Did you accidentally draw more than one black rule? Select each rule with the pointer and press Delete. Then start again with Step 3.

⑤ *Draw the rule under the 2" (8cm) ruler guide from the left to the right margin.*

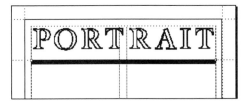

"Fit in window" size

6. Choose "Send to back" from the Element menu.

In the previous step, you drew the rule on top of the text. In this step you are telling PageMaker to put the rule behind the text. Then you'll see gray text on the black rule.

◆ If "Send to back" is dimmed, you may have deselected the rule before you chose the command. To remedy this, select the rule with the pointer and press Command + B (a shortcut for choosing "Send to back" from the menu).

7. Save your work.

Choose "Save as…" from the File menu to save your work with the name "Lesson 2." Giving the lesson a different name and choosing "Save as…" rather than "Save" keeps your work in Lesson 2 separate from that in Lesson 1.

⑥ *Choose "Send to back" from the Element menu.*

The text now appears in front of the rule

"Actual" size

⑦ *Save your work.*

Layering elements in PageMaker

Black box is behind white box; letter A is in front of white box

Black box is in front of white box

PageMaker places ruler and column guides, text blocks, and graphics in separate layers, somewhat like transparencies laid on an overhead projector. The object you worked with last is on the top; the object you worked with first is on the bottom or in the background.

Each time you select an object, PageMaker automatically makes it the topmost element. After you reposition an object, such as the black ID rule you made in the "Portrait" newsletter, you can send it behind the text by choosing "Send to back" from the Element menu, or you can use the keyboard shortcut, Command + B.

For more information on layering elements in PageMaker, refer to the technique "Working with multiple objects on the page" in the *Aldus PageMaker 4.0 Reference Manual*.

Placing the lead story

1. **Drag a horizontal ruler guide to 2-1⁄4" (9cm) from the top of the page.**
   When you place the lead story, you'll line up the top of the text block with this guide.

❶ *Drag a horizontal ruler guide to 2-1⁄4" (9cm).*

Saving disk space with "Save as…" and the same filename

Each time you save a document with the "Save" command, the changes you made since the last time you saved are added to the end of the file. Even if you delete text or graphics, the document may continue to grow in size.

When you save a document using the "Save as…" command, however, PageMaker compacts the file by discarding unwanted elements from earlier versions. The difference in file size can be striking, reducing file size by as much as 40%. So every now and then, after you've made significant changes in a publication, compress it by choosing "Save as…" from the File menu.

You can also use the "Save as…" command to create a copy of a document just as you have with Lessons 1 and 2. This can be useful if you're experimenting with the layout of a page, for example, and you want to save the existing version before trying another approach. In this instance, when you choose "Save as…" make sure you give the file a new name.

2. Choose "Place..." from the File menu. Select "Lead story" from the Lesson 2 box in the Tutorial folder and click "OK."

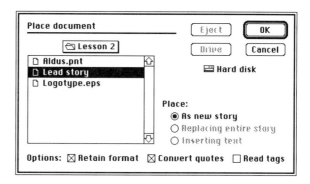

Choose "Place..." from the File menu and select "Lead story"

3. Position the loaded text icon at the intersection of the left margin and the 2-1/4" (9cm) ruler guide and click.

The lead story about Aldus Manutius flows to the bottom of the column. If the story looks like gray bars rather than text, it's because the font is too small for PageMaker to display on the screen in this page display size. Zoom in if you want to read the text.

◆ Did you put the text in the wrong place? You can move it. Using the pointer, click anywhere in the text and drag it to another location.

Position the loaded text icon and click.

The lead story flows to the bottom of the column

4. Check the position of the story in column 1.

You may want to switch to "Actual size" to make sure the text is flush with the bottom margin. If it isn't, drag the bottom windowshade handle using the pointer so text flows all the way down to the bottom margin. Now you're ready to place text in the second column.

5. Click the bottom windowshade handle.

This displays another loaded text icon.

6. Position the loaded text icon at the horizontal 2-1/4" (9cm) ruler guide in the next column and click.

The text flows to the bottom of the second column, though you may need to make the same adjustments you made in Step 4 above. The ▼ in the windowshade handle tells you there is more to the story, which you'll place on page 2 in Lesson 4.

◆ If you inadvertently placed the second column of text on top of text in the first column, press the Command key and, using the pointer, click in the overlapping text until you locate the misplaced text block. (Pressing the Command key while you click lets you select through layers.) When you have the text selected, drag it from *inside* the windowshade—*not* by the windowshade handles or the square handles—to a clear space on the page. Then position it as described in Step 6.

④ Check the position of the text.

The ▼ in the bottom windowshade handle shows there is more text to flow

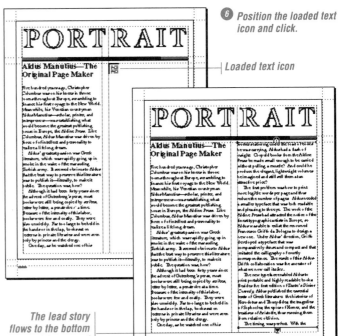

⑤ Click the bottom windowshade handle.

⑥ Position the loaded text icon and click.

Loaded text icon

The lead story flows to the bottom of the second column

Placing the Aldus graphic

1. **Choose "Place…" from the File menu. Select "Aldus.pnt" in the Lesson 2 box in the Tutorial folder and click "OK."**

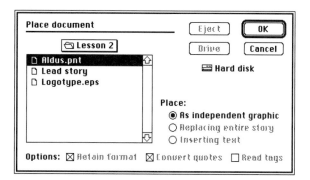

❶ *Choose "Place…" from the File menu and select "Aldus.pnt."*

2. **Place the paint-type icon on the pasteboard (outside the borders of the page) and click.**

   This places the graphic image on the pasteboard, outside the page. (The graphic is an image of Aldus Manutius, a 15th-century Venetian scholar, printer, and founder of the Aldine Press.) You'll position the image on the page in the next step.

❷ *Place the graphic on the pasteboard.*

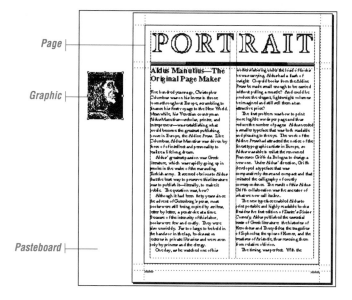

3. Using the pointer, select the Aldus graphic, and drag it to the intersection of the left margin and the 2-1/4" (9cm) ruler guide.

The graphic image is now on top of the text. In the steps that follow, you'll instruct PageMaker to wrap the text around the graphic.

◆ If you selected the text rather than the graphic, press the Command key while you click in the graphic until you select it.

③ *Drag the graphic onto the page.*

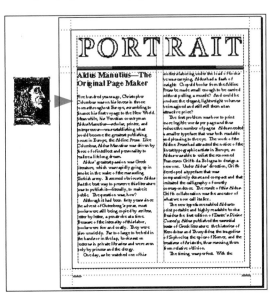

Graphic is on top of the text

"Actual size"

On your own

Placing a caption

If you have time, you may want to try placing a caption —*Aldus Manutius, 1450-1515*— beneath the image of Aldus Manutius. (If you add the caption, your screen will look slightly different from the illustrations in the next two lessons.)

1. **Using the pointer, select the graphic.**

2. **Drag the bottom boundary down (not the diamond handles in the corners).** This creates more space beneath the graphic image for the caption.

3. **Using the text tool, draw a small box below the image of Aldus Manutius in which to type the caption as shown here:** *Aldus Manutius, 1450-1515* Make sure the box does not extend beyond the boundary of the image. If it does, you won't get an insertion point.

4. **Select the caption, and center it by choosing "Align center" from "Alignment" on the Type menu.** You may want to use ruler guides to help position the caption more precisely.

You will need to adjust the text at the bottom of column 2 as you did when you placed the graphic. If you want to change the font and size, or italicize the caption, select it using the text tool and make your choices from "Type specs…" on the Type menu.

❶ *Select the graphic.*

❷ *Drag the bottom boundary down.*

❸ *Using the text tool, draw a small box and type the caption.*

Be careful; the box must be within the graphic's wrap boundaries

❹ *Center the caption.*

Wrapping text around the Aldus graphic

1. Choose "Text wrap..." from the Element menu.

Selections you make here will tell PageMaker how to wrap the text around the Aldus graphic.

2. For "Wrap option," select the middle icon.

3. For "Text flow," select the right icon.

4. For "Standoff in inches" (mm) change "Left" and "Top" to "0" (0mm). Change "Right" and "Bottom" to ".25" (5mm) and click "OK."

Press Tab to move from field to field. The standoff determines the white space around the image. You change "Right" and "Bottom" to .25 (5mm) to give a little more white space on those sides of the image; "Left" and "Top" are zero because you do not want text to wrap on that side.

After you click "OK," PageMaker wraps the text around two sides of the Aldus graphic.

◆ If nothing happened, you may have deselected the graphic image before you did Step 1. Using the pointer, select the graphic and begin again with Step 1.

◆ If you want to adjust the distance between the graphic and its boundary, drag the bottom dotted line up. Make sure you drag the boundary, not a handle.

5. Save your work.

① *Choose "Text wrap..." from the Element menu.*

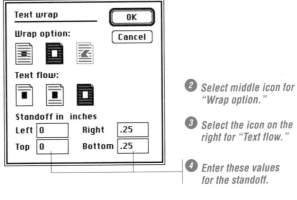

② *Select middle icon for "Wrap option."*

③ *Select the icon on the right for "Text flow."*

④ *Enter these values for the standoff.*

Graphic with text wrap applied

⑤ *Save your work.*

Introducing text wrap

If you haven't changed the PageMaker defaults, graphics you import and graphics you draw in PageMaker have no boundaries when you choose "Text wrap…" from the Element menu. There you specify either no boundary, a rectangular boundary, or a boundary you customize to follow the shape of the object. The graphic boundary appears as a dotted line on the screen and defines how close text can come to the graphic. It's displayed to help you edit, but it does not print.

If you want more information, see the technique "Customizing a graphic boundary" in the *Aldus PageMaker 4.0 Reference Manual*.

"Standoff" defines the distance between the graphic and its boundary

Wrap options determine the graphic boundary

No wrap deletes a graphic boundary; use this option to flow text over a graphic

Rectangular wrap creates a rectangular graphic boundary

Custom wrap sets up a graphic boundary that you adjust manually

Text-flow options (if you choose a graphic boundary)

Column break determines what happens when a graphic interrupts "autoflow" text

Text jumps over the graphic

Text wraps on any or all sides

What next?

You have now completed most of page 1: You created the masthead, placed the lead story, placed the image of Aldus Manutius, and wrapped the text around it.

In Lesson 3, you'll finish up page 1 of the newsletter by adding a table at the bottom of the second column. You'll use the story editor to edit the table, which you'll then place. Then you'll add a box with a black shadow behind it, commonly known as a drop shadow.

Before going on, make sure the newsletter looks like the one on page 74. If it doesn't, you'll find the next lesson easier going if you make the changes now. Don't forget to save your file before you proceed.

Lesson 3: Finishing page one

After Lesson 3, page 1 will look like this:

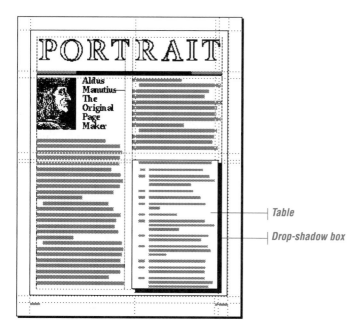

Table

Drop-shadow box

With most of page 1 completed, you'll put the finishing touches on now. You'll import a table ("A Brief History of Publishing") created in a word-processing program into PageMaker's story editor. There you'll make some changes to the table's content and place it into the newsletter. Last, you'll draw a box with a drop shadow around the table.

In this lesson you'll learn how to:

• Type and edit text in the story editor

• Place a story from the story editor onto the pasteboard

• Drag-place text

• Draw a box around text

• Create a drop shadow

What's in this lesson

Adding a table to the newsletter

First you'll import a table into PageMaker's story editor. You'll add a few lines to the table and make some changes using the story editor's "Change…" command. Then you'll place the table at the bottom of the second column on page 1.

The story editor and story view

You can edit text in PageMaker in either layout view or story view. Until now you've been using the text tool to type and edit text directly in layout view, which is the view of the page on the pasteboard. The text tool is efficient when you want to fit text into a particular space, because what you see on the screen is exactly how the text will print. (This is known as WYSIWYG: what you see is what you get.) Using the text tool is also the fastest way to make minor changes in text you've already placed on the page.

However, when you have lengthy blocks of text to type or edit, you'll want to take advantage of the story editor, a word processor within PageMaker developed to make text entry and revision fast and easy. The story editor will also make short work of such word-processing requirements as checking spelling, or finding and changing text. When you work in the story editor, PageMaker displays the story view, a text-only window placed on top of the layout view.

Story view gives you another view of your publication, in which changes you make are not displayed as they will actually appear when you print. In story view you look at the unadorned text, rather like glimpsing an actor in rehearsal, without makeup or costume. By ignoring graphics and most formatting, the story editor can speedily implement the editing changes you make to your document. In story view, the story (in this case, the table) exists only as an element of the publication, just as the role the actor plays exists only on the stage.

For more information on story view and the story editor, refer to the article "Story editor" and to the "Edit story…/ Edit layout…" command description in the *Aldus PageMaker 4.0 Reference Manual*.

Optional: Opening the file

• **Open the Tutorial folder and then the Lesson 3 folder. Last, open the "Lesson 2 done" file.**

If you're beginning with Lesson 3, open "Lesson 2 done" before proceeding. If you're continuing from Lesson 2, proceed with setting up the page for the table.

Setting up the page for the table

1. **Using the pointer, select the text block in column 2.**

As you work, make a habit of switching page display sizes whenever you need to change your perspective. Use close-up page display sizes, such as "200% size" or "Actual size," for detailed work, and "Fit in window" to give you the big picture. If you've forgotten how to change display sizes, return to page 40 in "Getting down to basics."

2. **Roll up the bottom windowshade handle to a little above the 4-1/2" (16cm) mark on the vertical ruler.**

This will create a space for the table. You will be working on the table in the story editor, so you won't really know how much space it will take on the page. It will be easiest when you return to the page if you guess on the generous side and make the space too big. You can always adjust the size of this text block after you place the table on the page.

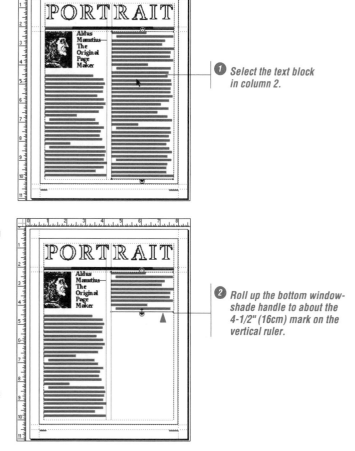

❶ *Select the text block in column 2.*

❷ *Roll up the bottom windowshade handle to about the 4-1/2" (16cm) mark on the vertical ruler.*

**3. Drag a horizontal ruler guide to the 5"
(17cm) mark on the vertical ruler.**
You'll use this guide later to place
the table from the story editor.

◆ If you need to reposition a ruler guide,
choose "Lock guides" on the Options
menu to turn off (uncheck) the
command. When you have finished,
choose the command again to turn on
"Lock guides."

**4. Drag out two vertical ruler guides,
one to 4-1/2" (11.5cm) and the other to
7-1/2" (18.5cm).**
You'll use these ruler guides later
to control the boundaries of the
table when you place it from
the story editor.

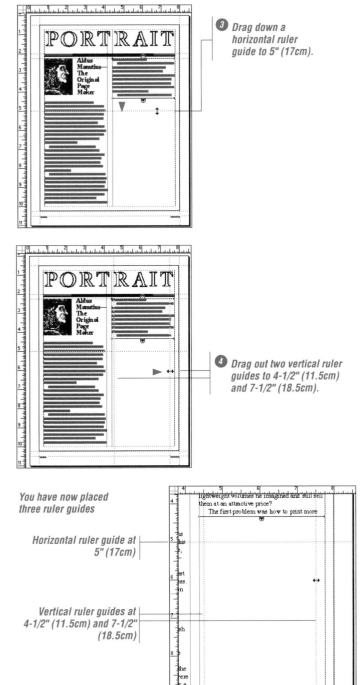

*❸ Drag down a
horizontal ruler
guide to 5" (17cm).*

*❹ Drag out two vertical ruler
guides to 4-1/2" (11.5cm)
and 7-1/2" (18.5cm).*

*You have now placed
three ruler guides*

*Horizontal ruler guide at
5" (17cm)*

*Vertical ruler guides at
4-1/2" (11.5cm) and 7-1/2"
(18.5cm)*

Importing the table into the story editor

Next you'll bring the table into the story editor, a word processor within PageMaker designed to make text entry and revision fast and easy.

1. **Select the pointer or text tool. Click outside the page to deselect the text.**
   Having no text selected ensures that you open an empty window in the story editor. If you select any part of the lead story using the pointer or click an insertion point in the text, the lead story will appear in the story window when you open the story editor.

2. **Choose "Edit story" from the Edit menu.**
   This command takes you to story view and provides you with a blank window into which to import the table.

3. **Choose "Import..." from the Story menu. Select "Table" in the Lesson 3 list box of the Tutorial folder and click "OK."**
   Use this command to import the table, which was created and for-matted in a word-processing program. Notice that, unlike the "Place..." command in layout view, the file flows automatically when you click "OK."

4. **Choose "Display ¶" from the Options menu.**
   This allows you to see tab markers and paragraph marks.

① *Select the pointer or text tool.*

② *Choose "Edit story" from the Edit menu.*

③ *Choose "Import...," select "Table," and click "OK."*

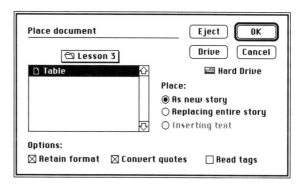

④ *Choose "Display ¶" from the Options menu.*

5. **Using the text tool, move the insertion point to the last paragraph mark in the table and press Return.**

When you press Return, you carry over the paragraph mark with all its formatting from the last line of the table. This ensures the next line will have the proper tab setting and the hanging indent format. You can't see the correct format in the story editor, but you will when you return to layout view.

6. **Add two more dates to the table, pressing the Tab key between the date and the descriptive text. Press Return at the end of each sentence.**

   1958 Photoelectric methods for controlling color registration and ink density are developed.

   1984 The introduction of Aldus PageMaker, the Macintosh computer, and the Apple LaserWriter printer usher in the era of desktop publishing.

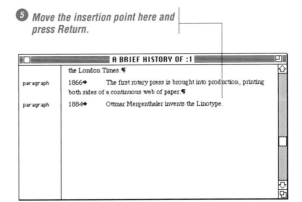

❺ Move the insertion point here and press Return.

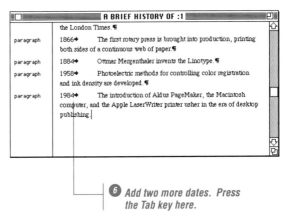

❻ Add two more dates. Press the Tab key here.

Why use the Tab key?

Text aligned by inserting spaces

Text aligned by inserting tab characters

Don't use the spacebar to line up text. The text won't line up properly because of PageMaker's precision character and line spacing. Instead, get into the habit of inserting tab characters (by pressing the Tab key) and using the tab ruler or the "Indents/tabs…" command on the Type menu. For more information about using the tab ruler, try the lesson "Setting indents and tabs" in this book or refer to the "Indents/tabs…" command description in the *Aldus PageMaker 4.0 Reference Manual.*

Do not press Return at the end of a line, as text wraps automatically to the next line. Adding these dates gives you a brief introduction to typing in the story editor.

Finding and changing a word

Using the "Change…" command in the story editor, you can find all occurrences of a word or phrase and substitute the text you want throughout an entire document. You can make the changes on a case-by-case basis or you can have PageMaker make all the changes automatically. In this table you'll make an editorial change: The writer used "press" several times and you're going to change that to "printing press."

For more information on the power of this command in the story editor, refer to the "Change…" command description in the *Aldus PageMaker 4.0 Reference Manual*.

1. Click the insertion point before the first letter of the table title.

This ensures that you start the search at the beginning of the table. You can also start a search at any point in the document: PageMaker begins searching at the insertion point and continues to the end of the story. Then PageMaker asks whether or not to continue the search from the beginning of the story. If you choose "Yes," PageMaker searches until it reaches the insertion point. When you start your search at the beginning of the story, you won't see this message.

2. Choose "Change…" from the Edit menu.

❶ *Click the insertion point before the first letter of the table title.*

	A BRIEF HISTORY OF :1	
paragraph	A BRIEF HISTORY OF PUBLISHING ¶	
paragraph	400➔	First known inked impressions on paper. ¶
paragraph	1440➔	Johannes Gutenberg develops the movable type printing press in Germany, cutting letters from an alloy of lead, tin, and antimony. ¶
paragraph	1449➔	Aldus Manutius is born in Padua. ¶
paragraph	1487➔	The Aldine Press is founded in Venice. ¶
paragraph	1501➔	The Aldine Press publishes Dante's Divine Comedy. ¶
paragraph	1515➔	Aldus Manutius dies. ¶
paragraph	1757➔	In England, William Baskerville publishes Virgil's Aeneid and Eclogues, using woven paper and a slender typeface. ¶

❷ *Choose "Change…" from the Edit menu.*

3. **Type** *press* **in the "Find what" box.**
   Press the Tab key to move to the
   "Change to" box and type *printing press.*
   You can further refine your search by
   asking PageMaker to look for whole
   words or words with a specific case.
   (In this example, you'll make the
   search more general, leaving "Match
   case" and "Whole word" unchecked.)
   You can also specify the text you want
   PageMaker to search: selected text,
   the current story (the story with the
   insertion point), or all the stories in
   a publication.

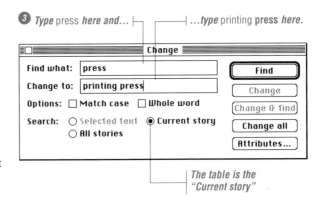

③ *Type* press *here and...* ⌐ ⌐ *...type* printing press *here.*

The table is the "Current story"

4. **Click "Find."**
   Note that PageMaker proposes you
   change "press" in "impressions." If
   you had checked "Whole word,"
   PageMaker would not have marked
   "impressions."

④ *Click "Find."*

PageMaker proposes that you change "press" in "impressions"

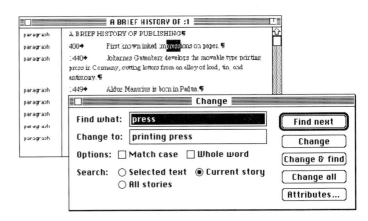

5. **Click "Find Next."**
   When you click "Find Next," you
   instruct PageMaker not to change
   "impressions" to "imprinting
   pressions." PageMaker leaves
   "impressions" as is and looks for the
   next occurrence of "press."

⑤ *Click "Find Next" to keep the text as is.*

6. Click "Change & find."

In this case you want to change "press" to "printing press." Clicking "Change & find" tells PageMaker to make the change and proceed with its search for the next occurrence of "press."

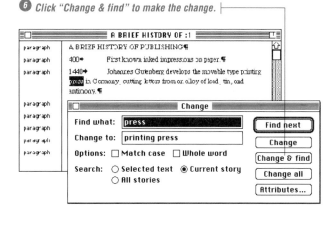

⑥ *Click "Change & find" to make the change.*

7. Repeat Step 5 or 6 until PageMaker has made all the changes you want.

Click "Find next" when you want to leave the text as is or "Change & find" if you want PageMaker to make the change. Note that PageMaker also finds "Press." Had you checked "Match case," PageMaker would have marked only words that began with a lowercase "p."

⑦ *Repeat Step 5 or 6 until you have made all the changes you want.*

8. When PageMaker tells you the search is complete, click "OK" and close the "Change" dialog box.

⑧ *Click "OK" and click here to close the "Change" dialog box.*

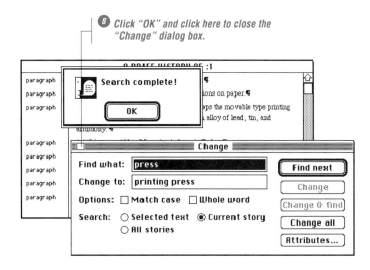

Positioning the table
in the newsletter

In the steps that follow, you'll place the table in the newsletter using a new technique, drag-placing. Then you'll adjust the table and the text above it so the table fits properly in the space.

1. **Choose "Place" from the File menu.**
   PageMaker returns you to layout view to place the table in the newsletter. No dialog box appeared because there is only one story you can place: the table you see in story view.

◆ If you click the close box, PageMaker responds with an alert box. Choose "Place" to return to layout view with a loaded text icon.

2. **Position the loaded text icon at the intersection of the 5" (16cm) horizontal ruler guide and the 4-1/2" (11.5cm) vertical ruler guide, but don't click yet.**
   You'll learn a new way to place text in the next step.

3. **Hold down the mouse button and drag the icon to the lower-right corner where the bottom margin and the 7-1/2" (18.5cm) vertical ruler guide intersect. Release the mouse button.**
   Placing text by dragging the mouse is called drag-placing. It requires a little skill and forethought, but rewards you with precise control over the placement of text.

❶ *Choose "Place" from the File menu.*

❷ *Position the loaded text icon here, but don't click.*

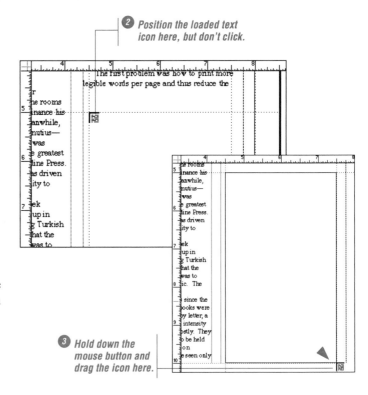

❸ *Hold down the mouse button and drag the icon here.*

◆ If you accidentally placed the table so you couldn't try drag-placing, simply roll the bottom windowshade handle up past the top windowshade handle. Then click the bottom windowshade handle to get a loaded text icon and try Steps 2 and 3 again.

4. Check the bottom windowshade handle to make sure you have placed the entire table.

If the whole table is not visible on the screen, drag the bottom windowshade handle down until it is. (If the text spills off the bottom of the page, you'll adjust that in the next step.) Notice, too, the text is now lined up properly in its hanging indent format.

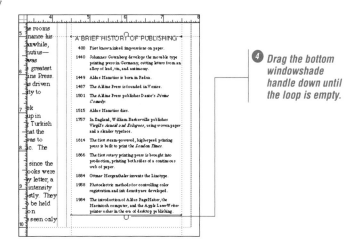

❹ *Drag the bottom windowshade handle down until the loop is empty.*

Why drag-place text?

When you place text on a page, PageMaker looks for a column to flow the text into. If it can't find a column, it flows the text between the margins. When you want to place text within margins or column guides, clicking the loaded text icon is the easiest method. But there will be occasions when these limits are too restricting. For example, for the table in this newsletter, you wanted to indent the text from the left column guide and the right margin to leave space for the box. In these instances, drag-placing is the answer: Set up ruler guides and pull the text within any boundaries you set.

5. Drag the table so the bottom edge of the table boundary is at the bottom margin.
This moves the text to the bottom of the column. The text may still overlap the text above it. In the next step, you'll take care of that.

◆ Did you forget how to move a text block? Using the pointer, click anywhere inside the text block and, holding down the mouse button, drag the table to the new location.

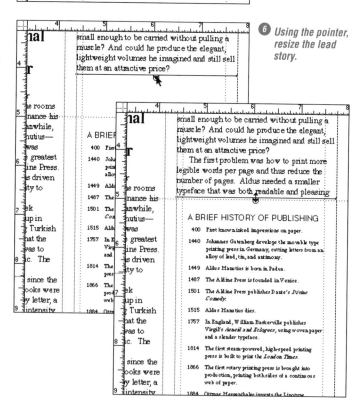

❺ *Drag the table to the bottom margin.*

Bottom margin

6. Using the pointer, resize the lead story so the bottom edge of its windowshade is within 1/4" (.5cm) of the top of the table text block.
This displays as much of the lead story on page 1 as possible. You'll find this task easiest if you use a close-up page display size so you can read where to break the page at a point that makes sense in the story. Notice that the sample text stopped at about 4-1/8 inches (15cm).

❻ *Using the pointer, resize the lead story.*

◆ Did you forget how to resize a text block? Drag the bottom windowshade handle down.

◆ Did you inadvertently display the loaded text icon? You probably clicked the windowshade handle instead of dragging it. To cancel the icon, click any tool in the toolbox.

7. Save your work.

Choose "Save as…" from the File menu to save your work with the name "Lesson 3." That way, if you take a break before you finish, you can easily pick up where you left off and the file will contain all your work to that point. Giving the lesson a different name and choosing "Save as…" rather than "Save" keeps your work in Lesson 3 separate from that in earlier lessons.

7 *Choose "Save as…" and name the file "Lesson 3."*

Using the grabber hand

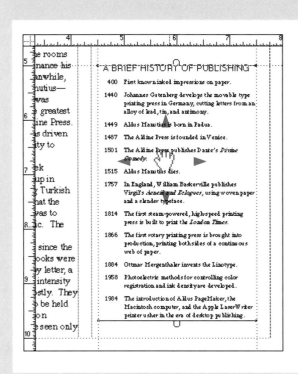

As you move back and forth between the bottom of the lead story and the bottom of the table, you might find the grabber hand useful.

Hold down the Option key and press the mouse button. The pointer changes to a tiny hand, the grabber hand. As you drag, the hand pushes the page in the direction you move the mouse, just as you would push paper around on a desk. When you release the mouse button, the hand changes back into a pointer.

Adding a drop-shadow box around the table

Next, you'll draw a box with a drop shadow around the table. To do this, you will create two identical boxes—one white and one black—and place them so the text block is on top, the white (or paper-colored) box is beneath the text, and the black box is below and slightly to the right of the white box.

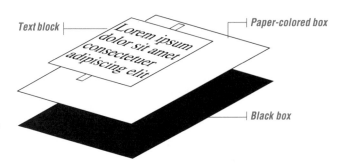

Text block | Paper-colored box | Black box

Drawing the first box

In these steps, you draw the first box, give it the color "Paper," and then put it behind the text.

1. **Choose "1 pt" from "Line" on the Element menu.**

   Choosing this line tells PageMaker how thick you want the border of the box to be.

   ❶ *Choose "1 pt" from "Line" on the Element menu.*

2. **Using the square-corner tool, draw a box around the table that is slightly larger than the text block.**

   When you move the square-corner tool onto the page, the pointer changes to a crossbar.

   ❷ *Using the square-corner tool, draw a box slightly larger than the table.*

   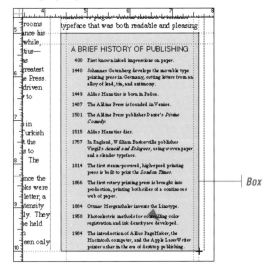

   Box

◆ Did you draw the box the wrong size or in the wrong position? You can resize the box by using the pointer tool to drag one of the box handles, or you can move the box. Or you can select the box using the pointer, delete it, and start over.

3. Choose "Paper" from "Fill" on the Element menu.

You choose "Paper" rather than "None" so the paper color will cover up the black box when you create it. The text disappears because PageMaker layers text and graphics, and the paper-colored box is now on top of the text.

◆ If nothing happens, perhaps the box was no longer selected. Using the pointer, point anywhere inside the box. Hold down the Command key and click until you see square handles and no windowshade handles. Then try Step 3 again.

4. Press Command + B.

This is the shortcut for choosing "Send to back" from the Element menu. The text is now visible because the paper-colored box is behind the text.

❸ *Choose "Paper" from "Fill" on the Element menu.*

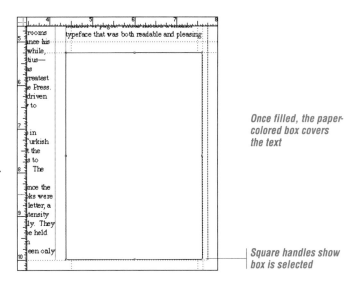

Once filled, the paper-colored box covers the text

Square handles show box is selected

❹ *Press Command + B.*

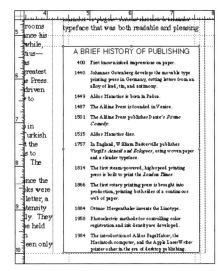

The paper-colored box moves behind the text

Copying the first box

To create the drop-shadow box, the two boxes should be the same size. The easy way to make them identical is to copy the box you just drew and then fill the copy with black.

1. **Point anywhere inside the table using the pointer. Press Command and click to select through the layers to the paper-colored box.**

   You'll know the box is selected when you see the square handles. If you see windowshade handles, you've selected the text layer and must click again to move to the box layer.

2. **Press Command + C.**

   This is the shortcut, similar to many Macintosh applications, for choosing "Copy" from the Edit menu.

❶ *Press Command and click until you select the paper-colored box.*

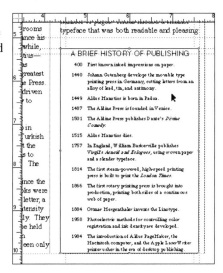

❷ *Press Command + C.*

On your own
Layering

Practice selecting and sending layers to the back with the three layers you've created in this lesson: the text layer, the paper-colored box, and the black box.

Select each layer in turn: Using the pointer, click in the box while pressing the Command key. When you've selected the boxes you'll see square handles on the corners; when you've selected the text you'll see windowshade handles.

As you select each layer, send it to the back by pressing Command + B. You can also bring a back layer to the front by pressing Command + F.

3. Press Command + V.

This is another Macintosh shortcut for choosing "Paste" from the Edit menu. You will now have a blank box floating on the page, obscuring the text.

③ *Press Command + V.*

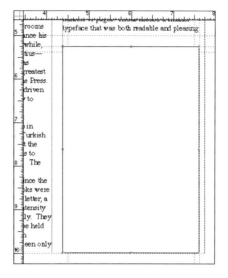

A copy of the box is pasted on top of the original box

◆ If you have a copy of the text instead of a box, you selected the text instead of the box. Delete the extra copy of the text and try Steps 1 through 3 again.

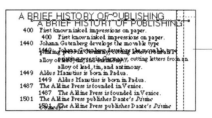

If you selected and copied the text block accidentally, the pasted-in block will look like a duplicated copy

4. Using the pointer, drag the box so that its lower-right corner is a little below and to the right of the first box.

Remember, you are creating a box that will be a shadow below and to the right of the text box.

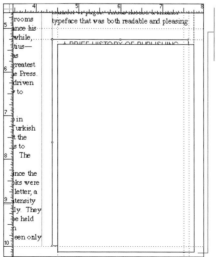

④ *Using the pointer, drag the box so that its lower-right corner is here.*

Making the second box black

1. Choose "Solid" from "Fill" on the Element menu.

The box becomes black.

◆ If nothing happens, it's because the box was no longer selected. Using the pointer, click the box to select it, and try Step 1 again.

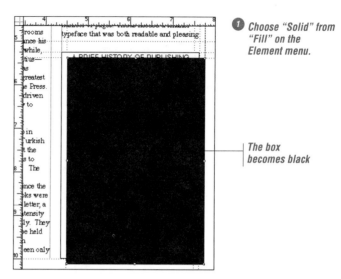

2. Press Command + B.

This command sends the black box to the back.

◆ If the black box doesn't look like this, you may have placed it incorrectly. You may select it and move it. Or, if you prefer to start over, delete it, and repeat the steps in "Drawing the first box" on page 106.

3. Save your work.

What next?

Now you've completed the first page of the newsletter. When you go on to Lesson 4, you'll lay out the second page of the newsletter. You'll do much of this on your own, practicing the skills from "Getting down to basics" and the first three lessons. It's a good opportunity to test your mastery.

Before going on, make sure the newsletter looks like the one on page 93. If it doesn't, you'll find the next lesson easiest if you make the changes now.

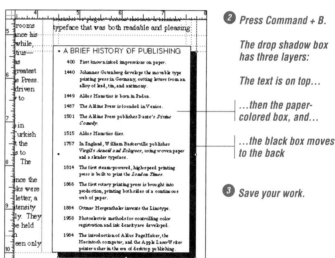

1 *Choose "Solid" from "Fill" on the Element menu.*

The box becomes black

2 *Press Command + B.*

The drop shadow box has three layers:

The text is on top...

...then the paper-colored box, and...

...the black box moves to the back

3 *Save your work.*

Lesson 4: Laying out the second page

When you've finished Lesson 4, your second page will look like this

Remainder of the lead story

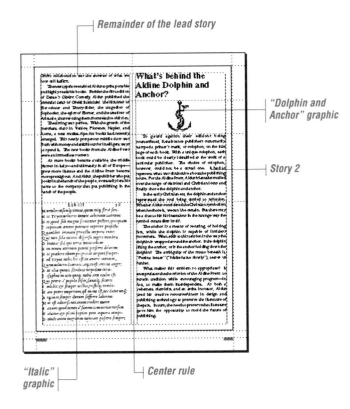

"Dolphin and Anchor" graphic

Story 2

"Italic" graphic

Center rule

Lesson 4 takes a slightly different approach from that of earlier lessons. You'll learn some new concepts, such as starting a new page and using styles to make formatting a publication easier and more efficient.

This lesson also asks you to repeat some things you've already mastered, such as placing stories and graphics on the page. When you get to those steps, you'll find them identified with "Almost on your own" after the title. We'll give you a summary of what you're going to do and a picture of what the newsletter should look like when you've finished. We've also outlined the general steps to follow if you need some help.

In this lesson you'll learn how to:

- Start a new page

- Use styles to format text

- Draw a rule in the center of a page

- Check the spelling in a publication

- Check letter and word spacing

- Print a proof and a final copy of your publication

What's in this lesson:

Placing the text on page 2

In this section, you'll create the second page for the newsletter. Then you'll place the remainder of the lead story in column 1 and the second story in column 2.

Optional: Opening the file

- **Open the Tutorial folder and then the Lesson 4 folder. Last, open the "Lesson 3 done" file.**

If you're begining with Lesson 4, open "Lesson 3 done" before proceeding. If you're continuing from Lesson 2, proceed with creating page 2.

Creating page 2

You specify the number of pages your publication will have in the "Page setup" dialog box when you open a new file. You can also add pages after you've started your publication, which is useful if your publication changes size in midstream.

The newsletter design specifies two pages, so you'll add the second page now.

1. **Choose "Insert pages..." from the Page menu.**

2. **Make sure that the "Insert pages" dialog box matches this one. Click "OK."**
   This inserts an additional page after page 1; page 2 appears on the screen.

1 *Choose "Insert pages..." from the Page menu.*

2 *Type 1 in the dialog box...*

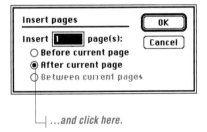

...and click here.

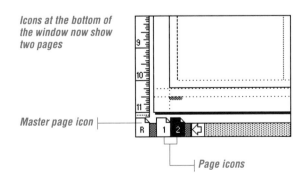

Icons at the bottom of the window now show two pages

Master page icon

Page icons

Placing the rest of the lead story on page 2

1. Click the page 1 icon.

This takes you back to page 1.

2. Using the pointer, select column 2 of the lead story. Click the bottom windowshade handle.

The loaded text icon appears, ready for you to place, or flow, text on the next page. You may find this easiest to do from the "Fit in window" page display size.

◆ As you work, switch display sizes when you need to change your perspective. Use close-up sizes, such as "200% size" or "Actual size," for detailed work, and "Fit in window" to give you the big picture. If you've forgotten how to change page display sizes, go back to page 40 in "Getting down to basics."

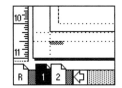

1 *Click the page 1 icon.*

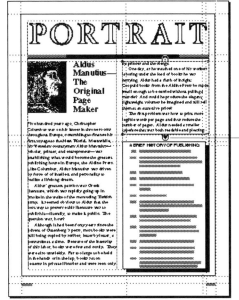

2 *Select the right-hand column and click the bottom windowshade handle.*

The ▼ in the bottom windowshade handle indicates there is more text to be placed

After you click, the loaded text icon appears

Moving from page to page

There are several ways to move from page to page in PageMaker. We've shown you one way in this lesson: clicking the page icon. This is easy to remember, but there are faster ways.

The fastest way to move a page or two at a time:

• Press Command + Tab to go forward a page
• Press Command + Shift + Tab to go back a page

The fastest way to move more than a few pages :

1. Choose "Go to page…" from the Page menu.
2. Type a page number and click "OK."

3. **Click the page 2 icon to return to page 2.**
The text icon temporarily changes to a pointer when you leave the page.

To return to page 2...

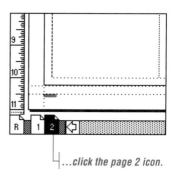

...click the page 2 icon.

4. **Position the loaded text icon in the upper-left corner of the page inside the margin guides and click.**
The remainder of the lead story flows onto the page. Remember, depending on the size of your monitor, the text on your screen may look different from that in the illustration.

Position the loaded text icon and click here.

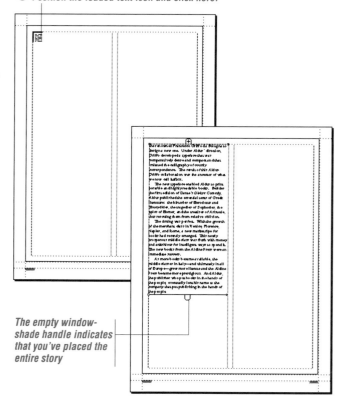

The empty window-shade handle indicates that you've placed the entire story

Placing Story 2: Almost on your own

Page 2 will look like this after you finish these three steps

In this section, you'll place the second story—a story about the symbol of the Aldine Press, an intertwined dolphin and anchor—in the right-hand column on page 2.

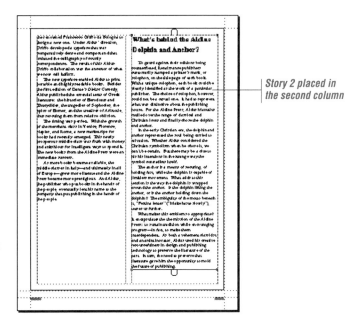

Story 2 placed in the second column

Try placing the second story on your own. Or, if you feel more comfortable, follow the steps below.

1. **Choose "Place..." from the File menu and select "Story 2" from the Lesson 4 list box. Click "OK."**

◆ If you've clicked an insertion point in the story using the text tool or selected a text block using the pointer tool, the File menu says "Replace..." Deselect the text and repeat Step 1.

2. **Position the loaded text icon in the upper-left corner of column 2 on page 2 and click.**

3. **Save your work.**
   Choose "Save as..." from the File menu to save your work with the name "Lesson 4." That way, if you take a break before you finish, you can easily pick up where you left off and the file will contain all your work to that point. Giving the lesson a different name and choosing "Save as..." rather than "Save" keeps your work in Lesson 4 separate from that in earlier lessons.

Formatting the text

You probably noticed that the stories you placed in the newsletter are already formatted. The body of each story is left-aligned, the type is 13-point Times, and the titles are larger (18-point) and bold. These stories were typed in a word-processing program, where styles were applied to each kind of text. The body of the stories has one style (named "Normal"), the titles have another style (named "heading 1"), and so on. PageMaker retained the styles stored in the word-processing document when you placed the stories in the newsletter.

In this section, you'll look at styles first and then change the style definition of both the body text and the titles.

What is a style, anyway?

A style defines the look of a paragraph in much the same way a costume defines the way an actor is perceived onstage. You can change styles as easily as an actor can change a costume, and the effect can be as profound.

Styles affect only the look of a paragraph, not its content. With one style you can control the font and its size, the type style (bold, italic), the alignment (centered, justified), and so on. Styles free you from having to apply several formatting attributes individually to each paragraph in your publication. For example, if you want all titles to be centered, bold, and underlined, you can apply all of those formats in one style, rather than having to apply each format to every title. As you will see, styles also make changing a format easy: You simply change the definition of the style and the changes are automatically applied throughout the publication.

Styles ensure that the style of each *kind* of paragraph remains consistent throughout the publication, a feature that is particularly compelling for use in lengthy documents. In this newsletter we have a style for body text paragraphs, and another style for the title paragraphs of the articles. We could also add a style for the title of the table you placed on page 1, the table text, or captions.

For more information on applying, modifying, and creating styles, refer to the "Style" command description in the *Aldus PageMaker 4.0 Reference Manual.*

Looking at styles

1. Choose "Style palette" from the Windows menu.

A small box appears which shows the list of style names defined for this newsletter; this is the "Styles" palette. If the "Styles" palette is not completely visible, move it by dragging its title bar.

◆ The "Styles" palette on your screen may vary slightly from the one in the illustrations. You can change the size of the "Styles" palette by dragging its size box.

2. Select the text tool. Click the insertion point in a title paragraph and then in a body text paragraph.

Notice as you move the insertion point from a paragraph with one style to a paragraph with another style that the style name changes in the "Styles" palette. This shows how different paragraphs can have different styles.

① *Choose "Style palette."*

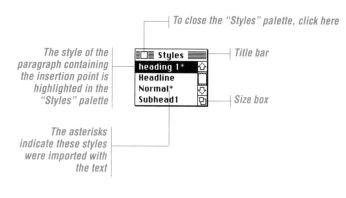

To close the "Styles" palette, click here

The style of the paragraph containing the insertion point is highlighted in the "Styles" palette

Title bar

Size box

The asterisks indicate these styles were imported with the text

② *Click the insertion point in different paragraphs.*

Title paragraph has been styled as "heading 1"

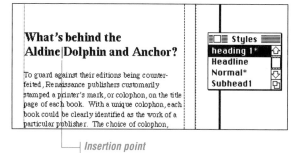

Insertion point

Body text paragraph has been styled as "Normal"

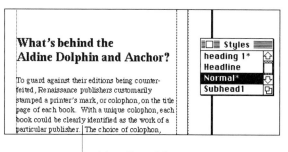

Insertion point

Changing the style of the body text

The body text was aligned left and set in 13-point Times. Text in newsletters is typically justified, so you'll change the alignment from left to justified. The font size is too large for the limited space in this newsletter, so you'll make it smaller, changing it to 12 points.

You could make these changes using the "Type specs…" command on the Type menu, but that would be tedious. You would have to format each story and each page separately, selecting every paragraph you want to change. Using styles, you can change the alignment and the point size for all the corresponding body text at once simply by changing the way the body text style is defined. The body text is styled as "Normal."

1. **Choose "Define styles…" from the Type menu.**
   You choose "Define styles…" because in the next several steps you'll change the way the body text style is defined for the whole newsletter. You'll work your way through a short succession of dialog boxes to specify first the font size and then the alignment.

2. **Select "Normal" and click "Edit…" in the "Define styles" dialog box.**
   Selecting "Edit…" tells PageMaker you're going to change the body text style.

3. **Click "Type…" in the "Edit style" dialog box.**
   In this step and the next, you'll change the type size to 12 points.

❶ Choose "Define styles…" from the Type menu.

❷ Select "Normal" and click "Edit."

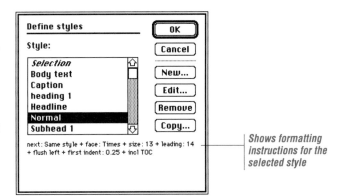

Shows formatting instructions for the selected style

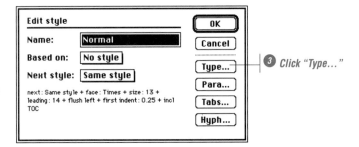

❸ Click "Type…"

4. **Change 13 (points) to 12 for "Size" in the "Type specifications" dialog box and click "OK."**

❹ Select 12 from the "Size" pop-up menu, then click "OK."

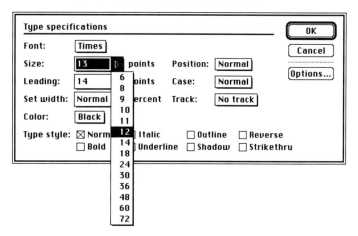

5. **Click "Para..." in the "Edit style" dialog box.**

   In this step and the next, you'll change the paragraph alignment to be justified.

❺ Click "Para..."

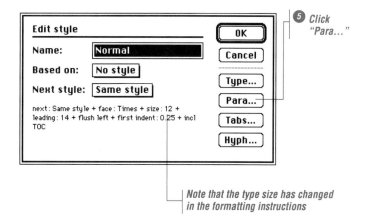

Note that the type size has changed in the formatting instructions

6. **Choose "Justify" for "Alignment" in the "Paragraph specifications" dialog box.**

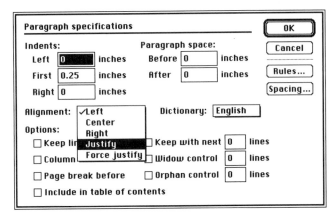

⑥ *Choose "Justify."*

7. **Click "OK" until you close all the dialog boxes and return to the newsletter.**

This closes the series of dialog boxes you just opened, instructing PageMaker to implement the changes you made. The changes ripple through the text. (If you can't see the difference in type size, switch to "Actual size" page display.)

⑦ *Close all the dialog boxes.*

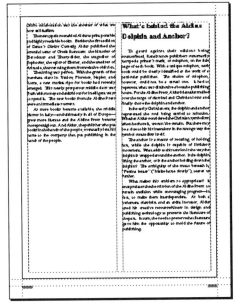

Page 2 should look like this

Changing the style of the titles: Almost on your own

You'll use the skills you just learned to change the style of the titles, the "heading 1" style. You'll change the font size from 18 to 24 points and the type style from bold to normal. When you've finished changing the style, the newsletter should look approximately like the second illustration.

Try to change the style definition on your own. Or, if you feel more comfortable, follow the steps below.

1. Choose "Define styles..." from the Type menu.

2. Select "heading 1" and click "Edit..." in the "Define styles" dialog box.

3. Click "Type..." in the "Edit style" dialog box. For "Size," type *24* in the "Type specifications" dialog box.

4. For "Type style," check "Normal."

5. Click "OK" to close the dialog boxes and return to the newsletter.

6. Save your work.

Titles as they were imported: 18 points, bold

What's behind the Aldine Dolphin and Anchor?

To guard against their editions being counterfeited, Renaissance publishers customarily stamped a printer's mark, or colophon, on the title page of each book. With a unique colophon, each

Titles after you change them: 24 points, normal style

What's behind the Aldine Dolphin and Anchor?

To guard against their editions being counterfeited, Renaissance publishers customarily

Placing and sizing graphics

In the next steps, you'll place two graphic images on the second page (the "Dolphin and Anchor" and the "Italic" graphics) and resize one of them. These are skills you have already mastered, so the steps below are intentionally sketchy to give you a chance to prove your mastery to yourself. If you need to review how to do a task, the page numbers in parentheses refer you to the pages in this tutorial that tell you how.

Placing the "Italic" graphic: Almost on your own

To place the graphic, "Italic.TIF," you'll need a horizontal ruler guide at 5-1/2" (14 cm). When you finish, the second page should look approximately like the illustration on the next page. (When first imported the graphic won't fit properly in the space. You'll resize it in the next section.)

Try placing the graphic on your own. Or, if you feel more comfortable, follow the steps below.

1. Drag down a horizontal ruler guide to 5-1/2" (14cm)(page 63).

◆ If you need to reposition this ruler guide, first be sure to uncheck "Lock guides" on the Options menu.

2. Choose "Place..." from the File menu and select "Italic.TIF" from the Lesson 4 list box.

Tiff icon

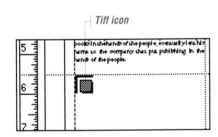

3. Position the TIFF place icon at the intersection of the left margin and the 5-1/2" (14 cm) horizontal ruler guide and click.

◆ It will be easier to position elements precisely on the page if you check "Snap to rulers" and "Snap to guides" on the Options menu.

Resizing the "Italic" graphic: Almost on your own

In this step, you'll resize the graphic you just placed, keeping the original proportions. When you finish these steps, the second page should look approximately like this.

Try resizing the graphic on your own. Or, if you feel more comfortable, follow the steps below:

1. Using the pointer, select the graphic.

2. Press Shift as you drag one of the corner handles until the graphic fits between the margins as shown (page 36).
Pressing Shift while you drag will ensure that PageMaker keeps the proportions of the original graphic as you resize it.

When you finish these steps, the second page should look approximately like this:

⊣ *Resized "Italic" graphic*

Creating a space for the "Dolphin and Anchor" graphic

In the next steps, you'll separate the body of the second story from its title to make space for the "Dolphin and Anchor" graphic image. You'll use a different method for creating space around a graphic than the one you used in Lesson 2.

1. Drag down a horizontal ruler guide to 3" (10cm).
This will serve as the guideline for placing the top of the text.

2. Using the pointer tool, roll up the bottom windowshade handle in column 2 until only the title is visible.

3. Click the bottom windowshade handle.
This gives you a loaded text icon containing the body of the story, which you'll place lower on the page.

◆ If you accidentally click the icon and place text on top of other text, roll up the windowshade completely of the text you just placed. Then try step 2 again.

4. Position the loaded text icon at the intersection of the left column guide and the 3" (10cm) horizontal ruler guide in column 2 and click.
This places the text so there's a space between the title and the body of the story.

◆ Is the "Styles" palette or toolbox obscuring your text? Remember, you can move or close them.

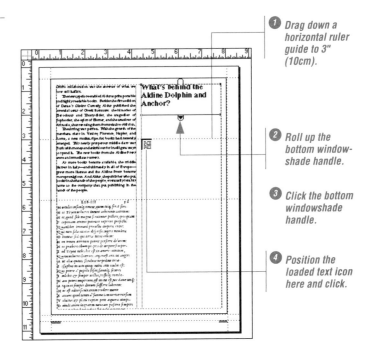

❶ Drag down a horizontal ruler guide to 3" (10cm).

❷ Roll up the bottom window-shade handle.

❸ Click the bottom windowshade handle.

❹ Position the loaded text icon here and click.

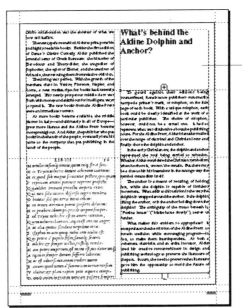

Space for the graphic

Placing the "Dolphin and Anchor" graphic: Almost on your own

In this section, you'll place the second graphic image, "Anchor.TIF," on page 2. The graphic is long, so place a horizontal ruler guide at 1-3/4" (6cm) to serve as the guide for placing the top of the image.

Try placing the graphic on your own. Or, if you feel more comfortable, follow the steps below:

1. **Drag down a horizontal ruler guide to 1-3/4" (6cm) on the vertical ruler (page 63).**

2. **Choose "Place..." from the File menu and select "Anchor.TIF" from the Lesson 4 list box.**

3. **Center the TIFF-type icon in the second column and at the 1-3/4" (6cm) horizontal ruler guide and click.**

4. **Adjust the position of the "Dolphin and Anchor" graphic if necessary (page 34).** Make sure the page on your screen matches the one in the illustration above. If it doesn't, make the necessary adjustments now.

5. **Save your work.**

When you finish these steps, the second page should look approximately like this

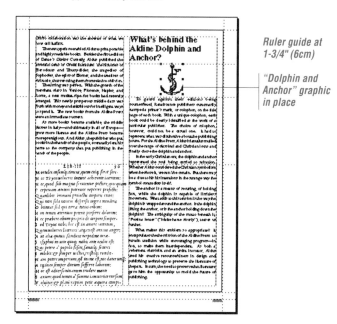

Ruler guide at 1-3/4" (6cm)

"Dolphin and Anchor" graphic in place

Fine-tuning the newsletter

The newsletter is almost finished. You'll want to appraise the results before you print the newsletter by asking yourself "Does it look the way I want it to?"

First, the newsletter needs a vertical rule in the center of page 2 to make it clear that the second story is not a continuation of the lead story. Checking spelling is always a good idea, as is checking the letter spacing. Then you'll be ready to print.

The newsletter will look like this just before you print it

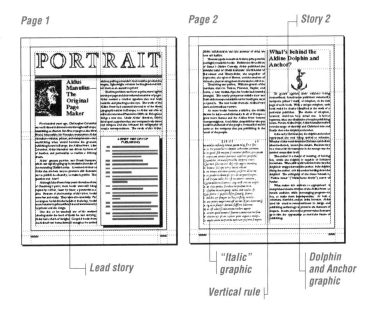

Page 1   Page 2   Story 2

Lead story

"Italic" graphic

Vertical rule

Dolphin and Anchor graphic

Use picas instead of inches

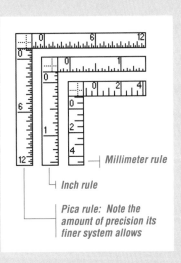

Millimeter rule

Inch rule

Pica rule: Note the amount of precision its finer system allows

You can avoid unwieldy fractions common to inches by using the measurement system of picas and points. This system of measurement, invented by Pierre Fournier in 1737, provides very small units of measure: 12 points = 1 pica; 6 picas = 1 inch (2.54cm). Picas, the measurement used for specifying type, afford a highly precise measuring system for margins, borders, and other page dimensions. It is the system used by typographers, typesetters, and designers.

To convert the measurements for this newsletter to picas and points at the beginning of the project, you would select "Picas" in "Measurement system" and "Vertical ruler" in the "Preferences" dialog box. This would change the default measurement. The ruler then displays picas rather than inches, and the dialog boxes with measurement options specify points or picas. (PageMaker, however, can override any of these defaults if you specify another unit of measure in any dialog box that requests a measurement.) If you had made the change to picas for this newsletter, you could use even measurements such as 37 or 45 picas for positioning the box without sacrificing accuracy.

Drawing a rule in the center of page 2: Almost on your own

In this step, you'll draw a 1-point line (or rule) down the center of the page.

Try drawing the rule on your own. Or, if you feel more comfortable, follow the steps below.

1. **Drag out a vertical ruler guide to 4-1/4" (10.75 cm) (page 63).**

2. **Choose "1" from "Line" on the Element menu (page 82).**

3. **Select the perpendicular-line tool.**

4. **Drag the crossbar down the ruler guide from the top margin to the bottom margin.** If the rule is difficult to see, zoom to a close-up page display size.

5. **Save your work.**

When you finish this step, the second page should look approximately like this

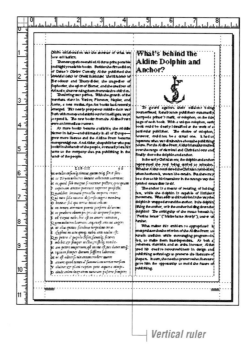

Vertical ruler

Checking spelling

PageMaker's new story editor has a full-fledged spelling checker that checks the spelling of words in the entire newsletter and proposes alternate spellings for words not found in the program's dictionary.

1. **Using the text tool, click the insertion point somewhere in the story on page 2.**

2. **Press Command + E.**
   This is the keyboard shortcut to get into story view where PageMaker will check your spelling.

3. **Choose "Spelling…" from the Edit menu in story view.**

   ◆ If you change your mind about checking spelling, click the close box in the "Spelling" dialog box.

4. **Click "All stories" in the "Spelling" dialog box, then click "Start."**
   This tells PageMaker to start checking the spelling for the entire publication from the insertion point.

➊ Click the text tool on some text.

➋ Press Command + E.

➌ Choose "Spelling…" from the Edit menu in story view.

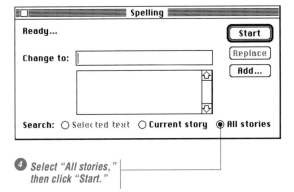

➍ Select "All stories," then click "Start."

5. Click the appropriate button for each word PageMaker displays in the "Unknown word" box.

Depending on where you click the insertion point when you begin to check spelling, you may not see the same text on your screen as in the illustration.

- Click "Ignore" to leave the word unchanged.

- Click "Replace" to correct a spelling error.

- Click "Add..." and make a selection from the list to add to the dictionary the words PageMaker doesn't recognize. You can also type the correct word in the "Change to" box if the correct spelling is not on the list.

6. When PageMaker displays the "Spellcheck complete!" message, click the close box.

7. Click the story view close box to return to layout view.

⑤ *Click the appropriate button for each word PageMaker displays.*

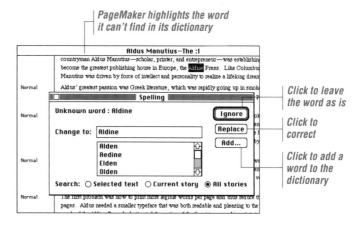

PageMaker highlights the word it can't find in its dictionary

Click to leave the word as is

Click to correct

Click to add a word to the dictionary

⑥ *Click the close box.*

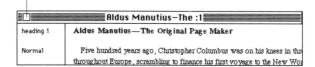

⑦ *Click the close box to return to layout view.*

More about checking spelling

The "Spelling…" command allows you to check spelling, punctuation, and syntax errors in a publication. The spelling checker highlights words it does not recognize, including both misspelled words and words not in its dictionary, such as Aldus Manutius. It also calls other errors to your attention, such as errors in capitalization or punctuation, or repeated words in a sentence (for example, "the the").

When you choose "Spelling," PageMaker checks each word in your publication against the words on its list. If PageMaker finds a match, it goes to the next word. If it doesn't find the word, it displays the word as "Unknown word," whereupon you can replace the word with your correction, ignore it, or add it to the user dictionary.

PageMaker maintains two dictionaries: a main dictionary which you cannot change, and a user dictionary to or from which you can add or remove words. Your user dictionary might contain specialized terms for your profession, acronyms, or the names of people and companies you work with.

Refer to the "Spelling… " command description in the *Aldus PageMaker 4.0 Reference Guide* for the fine points on checking your spelling.

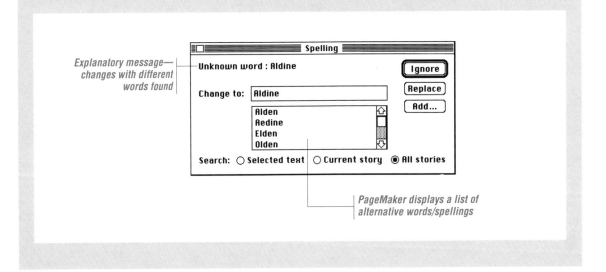

Explanatory message—changes with different words found

PageMaker displays a list of alternative words/spellings

Correcting letter and word spacing

Look at the first line of the story on page 2, "What's behind the Aldine Dolphin and Anchor?" (It's best to use "Actual size" page display size for this task.) You'll notice there's too much space between the letters and words. This is called a loose line. It results from conflicting formatting instructions to PageMaker. In this case, the combination of a narrow text block, justified text, and no hyphenation forced PageMaker to move "counterfeited" to the next line, thereby making the first line too loose.

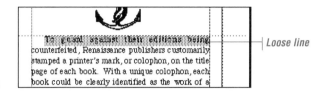

Loose line

The method for correcting a loose line is to hyphenate a long word on the line after the loose line, thereby defying wordwrap and forcing part of the long word to move back up to the loose line. In the steps that follow, you'll correct a loose line so the type is more evenly balanced.

For more information on correcting letter and word spacing, refer to the article "Spacing between letters, words, and lines of text" in the *Aldus PageMaker 4.0 Reference Manual*.

1. Chose "Preferences..." from the Edit menu. Check "Loose/tight lines" in the "Preferences" dialog box.
When you select "Loose/tight lines" from "Preferences" on the Edit menu, you instruct PageMaker to show the location of the loose lines. (A tight line is one in which PageMaker puts too little space between letters and words.)

1 *Check "Loose/tight lines" in the "Preferences" dialog box.*

```
Preferences                                    (    OK    )
Layout view:                                   ( Cancel )
   Measurement system:  [ Inches ]
   Vertical ruler:      [ Inches ]        [ 12 ]   points
   Greek text below:    [ 6      ]  pixels
   Guides:        Detailed graphics:    Show layout problems:
   ● Front        ○ Gray out            ☒ Loose/tight lines
   ○ Back         ● Normal              ☐ "Keeps" violations
                  ○ High resolution
Story view:
   Size: [ 12  ] ▷ points  Font: [ Times ]
```

2. Using the text tool, click the insertion point between *counter* **and** *feited* **in the word** *counterfeited.*

2 *Click the insertion point here.*

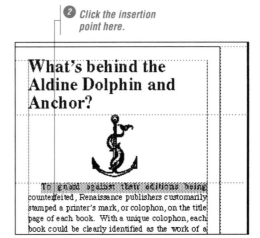

3. Press Command + - (hyphen).

Pressing Command + - (hyphen) forces some of the long word to the previous line to alleviate its "looseness" by creating a discretionary hyphen. A discretionary hyphen is one that prints only if the line breaks there. If you make changes later and the word no longer ends the line, you'll see the hyphen on the screen but it won't print.

3 *Press Command + - (hyphen).*

PageMaker alleviates the looseness of the line.

4. Save your work.

It's always a good idea to save your work before you print your publication.

4 *Save your work.*

Clearing ruler guide clutter

By now you have a forest of ruler guides on your pages. It is easy to remove them from view: Simply turn them off by choosing "Guides" from the Options menu. To restore the ruler guides, choose the "Guides" command again.

When you have finished using the ruler guides, you can clear them in one step by using "Copy master guides" from the Page menu. This removes all the ruler guides you placed on a particular page, leaving only the ones you specified on the master page.

Printing the newsletter

After you look over the newsletter onscreen, you're ready to print. First you'll print a proof copy for a last review on paper. (Research shows that, for whatever reason, people find errors more easily when they study a printed copy than when they look at the publication on the screen. Also, because graphics may take a long time to print, printing proof copies can save you time when you only want to proofread text.) Then, after editing your proof copy and making the final changes in PageMaker, you'll print a final copy.

1. **Choose "Print..." from the File menu.**

2. **Click "Options..." in the "Print to" dialog box.**

3. **Check "Proof print" in the "Aldus print options" dialog box and click "OK."**

① *Choose "Print..."*

② *Click here.*

```
Print to:  LaserWriter                    [ Print  ]

Copies: [1]      □ Collate  □ Reverse order    [ Cancel ]

Page range: ⦿ All  ○ From [1]  to [2]          [ Options... ]

Paper source: ⦿ Paper tray  ○ Manual feed      [ PostScript... ]

Scaling: [100] %  □ Thumbnails, [16] per page

Book: ○ Print this pub only  ○ Print entire book

Printer  [ LaserWriter Plus ]         Paper: [ Letter ]

Size:      8.5 H 11.0   inches    Tray: ⦿ Select
Print area: 8.0 H 10.8  inches
```

③ *Check "Proof print" and click "OK."*

```
Aldus print options                          [ OK ]

⊠ Proof print        □ Crop marks            [ Cancel ]
□ Substitute fonts   □ Smooth
□ Spot color overlays: [ All colors ]
□ Knockouts
□ Tile: ○ Manual     ⦿ Auto overlap [0.65] inches
□ Print blank pages

Even/odd pages: ⦿ Both  ○ Even  ○ Odd

Orientation: ⦿ Tall  ○ Wide    Image: □ Invert  □ Mirror
```

4. Click "Print."

PageMaker then prints a proof, printing only text and marking the graphics with placeholders.

◆ If you have problems printing, make sure the printer type in "Printer" matches the printer you're actually connected to. To check the current printer, choose "Chooser" from the Apple menu.

5. Edit your proof copy.

Make any changes onscreen and then save your work.

6. Choose "Print..." from the File menu. Click "Options..." and uncheck "Proof print," then click "OK."

You must tell PageMaker you don't want a proof print before you print a final copy.

7. Click "Print."

PageMaker prints a final copy of the newsletter.

④ *Click "Print."*

Print to: LaserWriter		Print
Copies: 1 ☐ Collate ☐ Reverse order		Cancel
Page range: ◉ All ○ From 1 to 2		Options...
Paper source: ◉ Paper tray ○ Manual feed		PostScript...
Scaling: 100 % ☐ Thumbnails, 16 per page		
Book: ○ Print this pub only ○ Print entire book		

Printer: **LaserWriter Plus** Paper: **Letter**
Size: 8.5 H 11.0 inches Tray: ◉ Select
Print area: 8.0 H 10.8 inches

Make sure the printer type named here matches the printer you selected in "Chooser"

⑤ *Edit your proof copy.*

⑥ *Choose "Print..." from the File menu. Click "Options..." and uncheck "Proof print," then click "OK."*

⑦ *Click "Print."*

What next?

You've now finished the newsletter and completed the main part of the tutorial. If you feel comfortable with the basic tools and techniques of PageMaker, try them out on a publication of your own or, if you're not entirely confident, go back and try "Getting down to basics" or Lesson 4 again.

The two lessons that follow in "Practice topics" are optional. After you have had some experience using PageMaker on your own, you may want to try them.

Setting indents and tabs

You'll practice setting a variety of indents and tab stops and then test your understanding by creating a bulleted list.

Unraveling threaded text

You'll add text within a story and outside it, delete text, break text blocks apart, and reorganize them.

Practice topics

These practice sessions follow the style of "Getting down to basics." Rather than concentrating on producing a document, you'll experiment with indents and tabs, and the flow of text from block to block. Don't worry about making mistakes.

These sessions assume you've had some experience using PageMaker to produce your own publications and are comfortable with the basic techniques and concepts of laying out text and graphics on the page. At the very least, you should have completed "Getting down to basics" before you tackle either of these sessions.

If you need help, read the notes marked with a small "◆" and look for page numbers in parentheses. They refer you to the pages earlier in the tutorial where you'll find additional instructions on how to do the task at hand.

Setting indents and tabs

If you're accustomed to using the spacebar to line up text on the page and have had some surprises, you'll want to get into the habit of using the Tab key and setting tab stops and indents using the "Indents/tabs…" command on the Type menu. In this session, you'll experiment with setting a variety of indents and tab stops and then test your understanding by creating a bulleted list. You'll practice:

- Indenting paragraphs from the margins

- Setting, moving, and clearing tab stops (right- and left-aligned, centered, and decimal)

- Defining and using leader characters

- Creating a bulleted list

What's in this lesson:

Setting indents

After opening PageMaker, you'll place a text file and use it to practice setting indents. We'll take you through the steps required to indent a paragraph from the left margin, indent the first line of that paragraph, and last, indent all the paragraphs in the document. Then you can explore other indent possibilities on your own.

Indenting text from the left margin

In the following steps you'll indent the first paragraph 1/2" (3cm) from the left margin and the first line 1/4" (1cm) more.

1. **Open the Tutorial folder and then the Indents & tabs folder. Last, open the "Indent practice" file.**

2. **Select the text tool and place the insertion point anywhere in the first numbered paragraph.**

① *Open the "Indents & tabs" folder. Double-click the "Indent practice" file.*

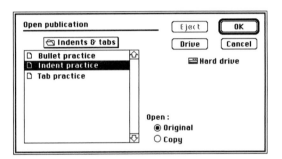

② *Place the insertion point anywhere in the first numbered paragraph.*

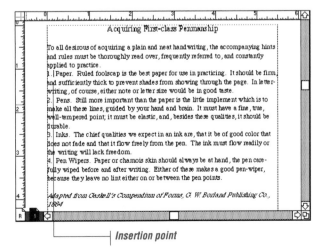

Insertion point

3. Choose "Indents/tabs..." from the Type menu.

Take a moment to study this dialog box.

◆ If the dialog box on your screen does not look like this, change your page display size to "Actual size."

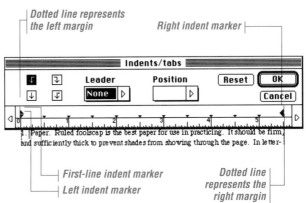

③ *Choose "Indents/tabs..." from the Type menu.*

Dotted line represents the left margin

Right indent marker

First-line indent marker

Left indent marker

Dotted line represents the right margin

4. Place the tip of the pointer on the lower triangle (the left indent marker) and drag it to the 1/2" (3cm) mark on the ruler.

This will indent the first paragraph 1/2" (3cm) from the left margin. Notice the first-line indent marker moves, too. This is because the left indent marker only moves in conjunction with the first-line indent marker. (The first-line marker, however, can move on its own without affecting the left indent marker.)

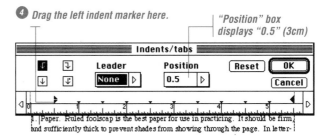

④ *Drag the left indent marker here.*

"Position" box displays "0.5" (3cm)

5. Place the tip of the pointer on the upper triangle (the first-line indent marker) and drag it 1/4" (1cm) more to the right.
This further indents the first line of the paragraph 1/4" (1cm). As you drag the upper triangle, keep your eye on the "Position" box as it notifies you of the indent marker's position.

⑤ *Drag the first-line indent marker 1/4" (1cm) more to the right.*

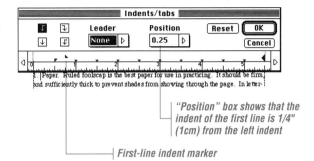

"Position" box shows that the indent of the first line is 1/4" (1cm) from the left indent

First-line indent marker

6. Click "OK."
Notice that only the first paragraph changed. This is because the insertion point was in just one paragraph. To apply the same indents to more than one paragraph, you must select them before you choose the "Indents/tabs…" command. You'll do this in the next step.

◆ If a different paragraph changed unexpectedly, the insertion point was in that paragraph before you chose "Indents/tabs…" To indent the first numbered paragraph, start again at Step 3.

⑥ *Click "OK."*

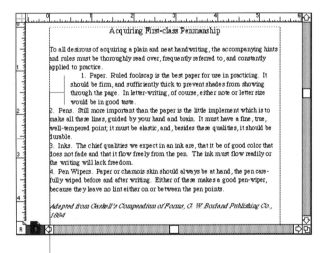

This paragraph is indented 1/2" (3cm) from the left margin; the first line is indented 1/4" (1cm) more

Indenting the remaining paragraphs

1. Using the text tool, select the paragraph you just changed and all the numbered paragraphs in the story.

◆ A quick way to select big blocks of text is to click in front of the first character you want to select and then hold down the Shift key and click after the last character you want to select. PageMaker selects all the text between the two characters.

① *Select all the numbered paragraphs.*

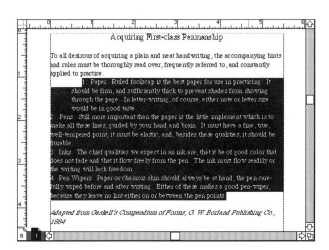

2. Choose "Indents/tabs…" from the Type menu and click "OK."
When you click "OK," PageMaker applies the indents from the first paragraph to all the paragraphs you've selected.

② *Choose "Indents/tabs…" from the Type menu and click "OK."*

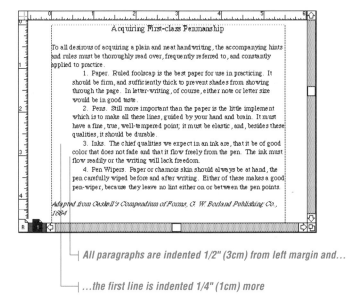

⊣ *All paragraphs are indented 1/2" (3cm) from left margin and…*

⊣ *…the first line is indented 1/4" (1cm) more*

Setting other indents:
Almost on your own

Now you can play with setting indents.
Try any or all of these practices.
When you have finished with each
step, your screen should look like the
corresponding illustration.

1. **Indent all the numbered paragraphs**
   1-1/4" (8cm) from the right margin.
   To indent text from the right margin,
   you will move the right indent marker
   to the left.

These paragraphs are indented
1-1/4" (8cm) from the right margin

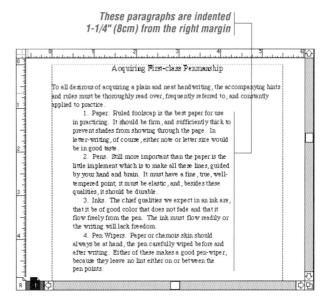

♦ If you can't see the right margin
marker, click the right scroll arrow
until the marker appears.

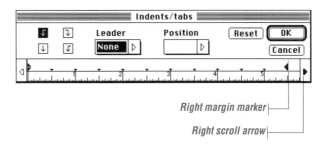

Right margin marker

Right scroll arrow

2. Indent all the numbered paragraphs 3/4" (4cm) from both margins.

You must set the first-line indents back to zero, in line with the left indent marker.

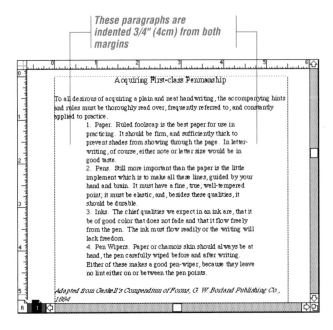

These paragraphs are indented 3/4" (4cm) from both margins

3. Indent only the first line of all the numbered paragraphs 1" (6cm).

You must set the right and left indents back to zero.

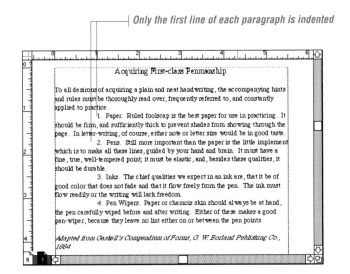

Only the first line of each paragraph is indented

4. Indent all but the first line of all the numbered paragraphs 1/2" (3cm) from the left margin.

Remember, you can only move the left indent marker in conjunction with the first-line indent marker.

When the first line of a paragraph "hangs" out to the left of the remaining lines, it's called a hanging indent. For more general information on hanging indents, refer to the technique, "Setting a hanging indent" in the *Aldus PageMaker 4.0 Reference Manual*.

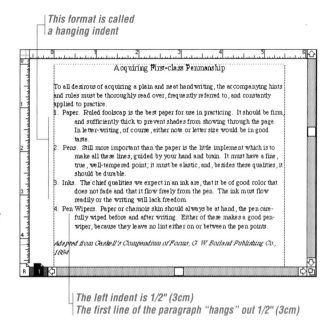

This format is called a hanging indent

The left indent is 1/2" (3cm)
The first line of the paragraph "hangs" out 1/2" (3cm)

5. When you have finished, close the file without saving the changes.

Inserting tabs and setting tab stops

In this section, you'll add two lines to a table, set a decimal tab stop and a left-aligned tab stop, insert a leader character, and change a tab stop. On your own you'll set a left-aligned tab stop and change a right-aligned tab stop.

Before tabs and leaders are set

Long Bridges of the World (in miles)

1	Seto-Ohashi, Honshu to Shikoku, Japan	7.9
2	Huey P. Long, Louisiana, U.S.A.	4.35530
3	Yangtse River, Nanjing, China	4.2
4	Mackinac Straits, Michigan, U.S.A. 3.63	
5	Lake Washington, Washington, U.S.A.	2.385606

After tabs and leaders are set

Long Bridges of the World (in miles)

1	Seto-Ohashi, Honshu to Shikoku, Japan	7.9
2	Huey P. Long, Louisiana, U.S.A.	4.35530
3	Yangtse River, Nanjing, China	4.2
4	Mackinac Straits, Michigan, U.S.A.	3.63
5	Lake Washington, Washington, U.S.A.	2.385606
6	Akashi-Kaikyo, Honshu to Shikoku, Japan	2.212
7	Messina, Sicily, to the mainland, Italy	2.0628

Opening the practice file

1. Open the "Tab practice" file in the Indents & tabs list box.

2. Go to "Actual size" page display size.
In this display size, you can read the text. If necessary, scroll to see the entire document. Don't let the jumbled state of the table "Long Bridges of the World" bother you; the purpose of this exercise is to give the table some order by setting tab stops.

❶ *Open the "Tab practice" file in the Indents & tabs list box.*

❷ *Go to "Actual size."*

Long Bridges of the World (in miles)

1	Seto-Ohashi, Honshu to Shikoku, Japan	7.9
2	Huey P. Long, Louisiana, U.S.A.	4.35530
3	Yangtse River, Nanjing, China	4.2
4	Mackinac Straits, Michigan, U.S.A. 3.63	
5	Lake Washington, Washington, U.S.A.	2.385606

"Actual size"

Adding text to the table

● **Using the text tool, add the following two lines to the bottom of the table you just placed:**

> 6 *Akashi-Kaikyo, Honshu to Shikoku, Japan*   *2.212*

> 7 *Messina, Sicily, to the mainland, Italy*   *2.0628*

Press the Tab key to insert a tab character between the number and the bridge name, and between the bridge name and its length.

◆ To see the tab characters you are inserting, read "Seeing is believing" in the box below to learn how to make them visible.

• *Add two lines to the table.*

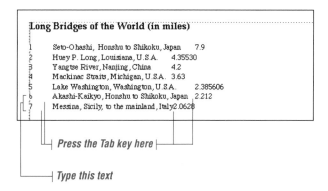

| Press the Tab key here |

| Type this text |

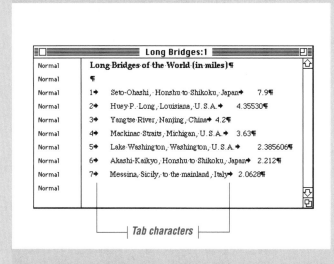

Seeing is believing

| Tab characters |

When you press the Tab key, you may feel you are typing a phantom character. But tab characters, although invisible, are essential to making a table work. If you want to see the tab characters, put the table in story view. To do this, select the text tool and click an insertion point somewhere in the table. Choose "Edit story" from the Edit menu. Once in the story editor, choose "Display ¶" from the Options menu and the tab characters will appear.

Take this opportunity to check the tab characters. You should have two on each line. If you don't, insert them now as shown in the illustration. Return to layout view by clicking the story editor close box.

Setting tab stops

In this section you'll set a decimal tab
stop and a left-aligned tab stop.

**1. Using the text tool, select the entire table
except the title.**

You select the whole table because
you want to change tab stops in
every line.

1 *Select the entire table except the title.*

**2. Choose "Indents/tabs..." from the Type
menu.**

2 *Choose "Indents/tabs..." from the Type menu.*

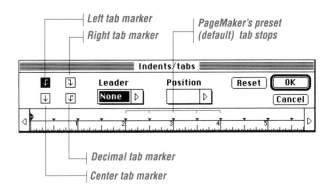

Left tab marker
Right tab marker
PageMaker's preset
(default) tab stops

Decimal tab marker
Center tab marker

**3. Select the decimal tab marker and click
the ruler at 4" (12cm).**

This sets the tab stop to align the
column of numbers at the decimal.
The "Indents/tabs" dialog box
confirms this by indicating "4" (12cm)
in the "Position" box. Notice that
when you set the tab stops, PageMaker
clears all the default tab stops to the
left of the one you set.

◆ If you didn't get the tab marker in
quite the right place, drag it along
the ruler line until it is in the correct
position. If you want to start over, you
can delete the tab marker by dragging
it down and out of the dialog box.

3 *Select the decimal tab marker and click the ruler at 4" (12cm).*

"Position" box displays "4" (12cm)

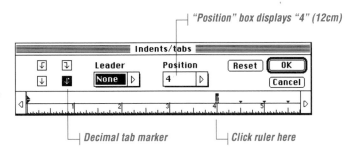

Decimal tab marker
Click ruler here

4. Select the left tab marker and click the ruler at 1/4" (1cm).

This tab stop will line up the bridge names and locations.

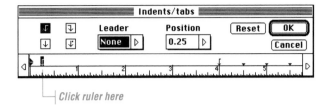

Select the left tab marker and click the ruler at 1/4" (1cm).

Click ruler here

Making tables easy

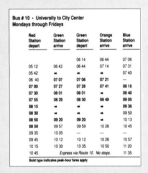

Each line of the "Long Bridges of the World" table was created by pressing the Return key to make a new paragraph and a new line. You may have noticed by now that before you set indents and tabs for one paragraph, you need only move the insertion point to that paragraph. If, however, you want to format more than one paragraph, you must first select all the paragraphs you want to format.

If you press Shift + Return at the end of each line instead of pressing only Return, PageMaker will create a new line but within the existing paragraph. Then, rather than selecting the table, you only need move the insertion point in the table before applying indents and tabs to the entire table.

But remember, when you create more complex tables you will want to take advantage of PageMaker's Table Editor. For ideas and information about how to use the Table Editor, refer to the *Table Editor Guide*.

5. Click "OK."

◆ If the layout of the table does not change, you may not have selected the table before choosing "Indents/tabs..." Select the table and repeat Steps 2 through 5.

◆ Are the last two lines of text not properly aligned? You may have forgotten to insert tab characters between the name of the bridge and its length. Follow the directions in Step 1 for adding tab stops to the table and then reformat the tab stops.

Changing tab stops: Almost on your own

Moving a tab stop is as simple as sliding the tab marker along the ruler to the new position. Changing the alignment of a tab stop is almost as easy. For example, to change the decimal-aligned tab stop in the table to a right-aligned tab stop, follow these steps:

1. Using the text tool, select the paragraphs you want to change.

2. Choose "Indents/tabs..." from the Type menu and select the decimal-aligned tab marker that is already on the ruler.

3. Click the right tab marker and click "OK." That's it. The numbers are no longer aligned at the decimal. This might not be the kind of format you'd normally use for these numbers, but it's useful for page numbers in a table of contents or an index, for example.

❺ *Click "OK."*

Long Bridges of the World (in miles)

1	Seto-Ohashi, Honshu to Shikoku, Japan	7.9
2	Huey P. Long, Louisiana, U.S.A.	4.35530
3	Yangtse River, Nanjing, China	4.2
4	Mackinac Straits, Michigan, U.S.A.	3.63
5	Lake Washington, Washington, U.S.A.	2.385606
6	Akashi-Kaikyo, Honshu to Shikoku, Japan	2.212
7	Messina, Sicily, to the mainland, Italy	2.0628

After you've finished these steps, the numbers will be aligned on the right

Long Bridges of the World (in miles)

1	Seto-Ohashi, Honshu to Shikoku, Japan	7.9
2	Huey P. Long, Louisiana, U.S.A.	4.35530
3	Yangtse River, Nanjing, China	4.2
4	Mackinac Straits, Michigan, U.S.A.	3.63
5	Lake Washington, Washington, U.S.A.	2.385606
6	Akashi-Kaikyo, Honshu to Shikoku, Japan	2.212
7	Messina, Sicily, to the mainland, Italy	2.0628

Inserting a leader character

The table might be easier to read if there were a line of dots between the name and location of the bridge and its length. This line of dots is called a leader because it leads your eye across the page. Follow these steps to insert a leader character in each row of the table.

1. **Using the text tool, select the whole table except the title.**

2. **Choose "Indents/tabs..." from the Type menu.**

3. **Select the right tab marker that is already on the ruler (not the tab marker to the left of the leader box).**
   The "Leader" edit box says "None," indicating that no leaders are selected.

◆ If there is no right tab marker on the ruler, you selected the title of the table, too. Start over with Step 1.

4. **Press on the arrow just to the right of the "Leader" box.**
   When you press the mouse button, a list of leader-character styles pops up.

❶ *Using the text tool, select the whole table except the title.*

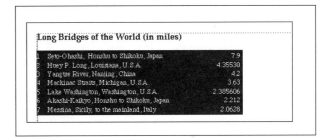

❷ *Choose "Indents/tabs..." from the Type menu.*

❸ *Select the right tab marker that is already on the ruler.*

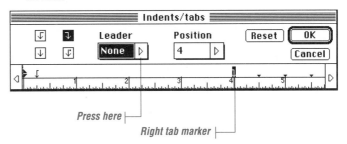

❹ *Press on the arrow to the right of the "Leader" box.*

5. Choose the periods and click "OK."

⑤ Choose the periods and click "OK."

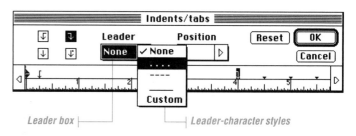

Leader box ⌐ | ⌐ Leader-character styles

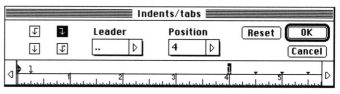

Long Bridges of the World (in miles)

1 Seto-Ohashi, Honshu to Shikoku, Japan 7.9
2 Huey P. Long, Louisiana, U.S.A. 4.35530
3 Yangtse River, Nanjing, China...4.2
4 Mackinac Straits, Michigan, U.S.A................................3.63
5 Lake Washington, Washington, U.S.A. 2.385606
6 Akashi-Kaikyo, Honshu to Shikoku, Japan........................2.212
7 Messina, Sicily, to the mainland, Italy 2.0628

6. Close the file without saving it.

⑥ Close the file without saving it.

Creating a custom leader character

Type "--" in the "Leader" box to get this leader character

Long Bridges of the World (in miles)

1 Seto-Ohashi, Honshu to Shikoku, Japan -------------- 7.9
2 Huey P. Long, Louisiana, U.S.A. -------------------- 4.35530
3 Yangtse River, Nanjing, China --------------------- 4.2
4 Mackinac Straits, Michigan, U.S.A.----------------- 3.63
5 Lake Washington, Washington, U.S.A---------------- 2.385606
6 Akashi-Kaikyo, Honshu to Shikoku, Japan------------ 2.212
7 Messina, Sicily, to the mainland, Italy -------------- 2.0628

You can design your own leaders. Choose "Custom" from the "Leader" pop-up menu and type the leader character of your choice twice in the "Leader" box. (Remember, for a dotted leader, there were two dots.)

Creating a bulleted list: Almost on your own

In this exercise, you'll put your knowledge of indents and tabs together to format a bulleted list.

You'll find this exercise easiest to do from the "Actual size" page display size.

1. **Open the file "Bullet practice" in the "Indents & tabs" folder.**

    When the file was typed, a tab was inserted between the bullet and the information about each astronaut.

2. **Using the text tool, indent all but the first line of each bulleted paragraph 3/4" (8cm) from the left margin.**

3. **Indent the first line of each bulleted paragraph 1/2" (6cm) from the left margin.**

4. **Set a left tab stop 3/4" (8cm) from the left margin and click "OK."**

5. **Close the file without saving the changes.**

The bulleted list before formatting

Astronaut Statistics

Space beyond earth has always fascinated human beings, but it has only been recently that men and women have been able to break the bonds of Planet Earth.

• The first astronaut was Col Yuriy Gagarin (USSR), April 12, 1961.
• The first woman astronaut was Lt-Col Valentina Vladinirovna Tereshkova (USSR), June 16, 1963.
• The first person to walk in space was Lt-Col Aleksey A. Leonov (USSR), March 18, 1965.
• The first person to walk on Earth's moon was Neil A. Armstrong (USA), July 21, 1969.
• The first woman to walk in space was Madame Svetlana Savitskaya-Khatkovsky (USSR), July 25, 1984.
• Capt. John Watts Young (USA), who completed the most journeys: six space flights totalling 34 days, 19 hours, 42 minutes, and 13 seconds.

The bulleted list after setting the indents and tabs

Astronaut Statistics

Space beyond earth has always fascinated human beings, but it has only been recently that men and women have been able to break the bonds of Planet Earth.

- The first astronaut was Col Yuriy Gagarin (USSR), April 12, 1961.
- The first woman astronaut was Lt-Col Valentina Vladinirovna Tereshkova (USSR), June 16, 1963.
- The first person to walk in space was Lt-Col Aleksey A. Leonov (USSR), March 18, 1965.
- The first person to walk on Earth's moon was Neil A. Armstrong (USA), July 21, 1969.
- The first woman to walk in space was Madame Svetlana Savitskaya-Khatkovsky (USSR), July 25, 1984.
- Capt. John Watts Young (USA), who completed the most journeys: six space flights totalling 34 days, 19 hours, 42 minutes, and 13 seconds.

What next?

You may want to experiment further or read more information on indents and tabs in the "Indents/tabs…" command description in the *Aldus PageMaker 4.0 Reference Manual.*

Unraveling threaded text

When you place a file, PageMaker considers it to be a story (in contrast to a publication, which may contain many stories). The story, if very brief, may be contained in one text block; for example, it might be a headline or a simple two-line advertisement. However, stories are often longer than one text block. The number and size of the text blocks are controlled partly by the margins and column guides and partly by how you place the text on the page. The longest a text block can be—as opposed to a story—is one column.

This session elaborates on one of the most fundamental concepts in PageMaker: how text flows within a story from one text block to another. Simple enough on the surface, text flow is a powerful feature that lets you break a single story into as many blocks as you want while keeping the flow of the story from block to block intact. This practice session contains some basic information about the way PageMaker flows—or threads—text from one text block to another. You'll add text within a story and outside it; you'll delete text, break text blocks apart, and reorganize them. You'll practice:

- Identifying a text block and threaded text in a story

- Expanding and shrinking text blocks

- Creating and reorganizing text blocks

- Adding text within a text block

- Threading and unthreading text

What's in this lesson

Changing the size of text blocks

As you work with text blocks in these and subsequent steps, you'll learn how text flows from block to block. Each text block is somewhat like a car on a train. Adding a car—or ten cars—does not affect the coupling of the other cars and they all move forward on the rail. If you remove a car, the whole train becomes shorter.

However, unlike cars on a train, the content of the text blocks in PageMaker is connected too, as if by a pipe. When you add, move, or remove text within a block, the effects of the change ripple through the rest of the blocks. When you reorganize text blocks, they remain linked by their pipelines: PageMaker tracks the original order of the text blocks so that text flows from block to block in its original order even though the blocks may have moved to a new position or become a new size or shape.

The following exercises will give you a working familiarity with the way text flows from block to block in PageMaker. You'll watch the impact on text of expanding and shrinking text blocks, and you'll see how the changes you make to the text in one text block affect subsequent text blocks.

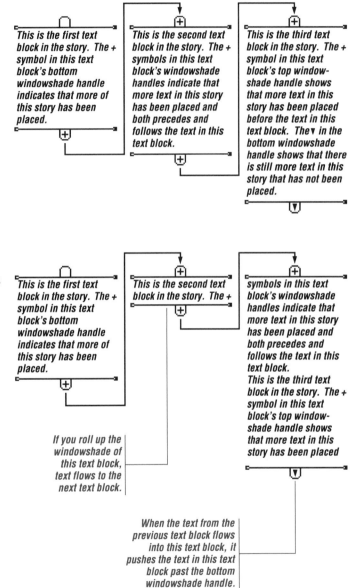

This is the first text block in the story. The + symbol in this text block's bottom windowshade handle indicates that more of this story has been placed.

This is the second text block in the story. The + symbols in this text block's windowshade handles indicate that more text in this story has been placed and both precedes and follows the text in this text block.

This is the third text block in the story. The + symbol in this text block's top windowshade handle shows that more text in this story has been placed before the text in this text block. The ▼ in the bottom windowshade handle shows that there is still more text in this story that has not been placed.

This is the first text block in the story. The + symbol in this text block's bottom windowshade handle indicates that more of this story has been placed.

This is the second text block in the story. The +

symbols in this text block's windowshade handles indicate that more text in this story has been placed and both precedes and follows the text in this text block.
This is the third text block in the story. The + symbol in this text block's top windowshade handle shows that more text in this story has been placed

If you roll up the windowshade of this text block, text flows to the next text block.

When the text from the previous text block flows into this text block, it pushes the text in this text block past the bottom windowshade handle.

Opening the practice file

1. Open PageMaker.

2. Choose "Open..." from the File menu and select "Threading 1" in the Threading list box of the Tutorial folder.

3. Click "Copy" in the "Open publication" dialog box and click "OK."
This creates a copy of the file "Threading 1" so if you lose sight of the original order of things, you can close the publication and open "Threading 1" again for a fresh start. We've numbered the paragraphs in "Threading 1" so you can clearly see the impact of your experiments. Note that what you see on your screen may be slightly different from the illustrations in this session, depending on the size of your screen.

4. Save the file as "Threading practice 1."
This gives the copy a name.

❶ Open PageMaker.

❷ Choose "Open..." from the File menu and select "Threading 1."

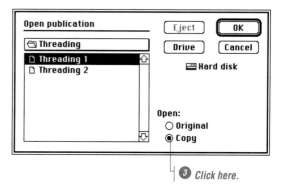

❸ Click here.

❹ Save the file as "Threading practice 1."

Expanding and shrinking a text block

Suppose you've placed some text on a page and now you want to make space for a graphic image or text not in the current story. You can do this easily in PageMaker by shrinking a text block. In this section, you'll experiment with the play of text between text blocks as you expand and shrink them.

You'll find most of these tasks easiest to do from "Fit in window" page display size. If you want to read the text, switch to "Actual size" or larger. You will also find that some of the upcoming experiments require you to switch from one page display size to another, particularly between "Fit in window" and "Actual size." For a reminder on the most efficient way to do this, see page 40 earlier in this book.

The anatomy of a windowshade handle

The windowshade handle of a text block selected using the pointer can tell you a lot when you know how to interpret the symbols.

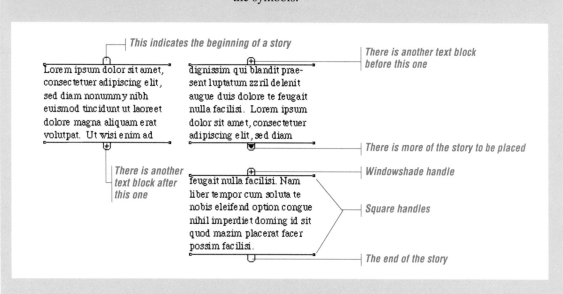

1. Using the pointer, select first one column, and then the other.

This story is made up of two text blocks: one in column 1, the other in column 2. Each text block is bounded by windowshade handles, aptly named because you use them to raise or lower the boundaries of the text block in the same way you raise or lower a windowshade. In fact, raising the handle is called "rolling up the windowshade."

2. Select column 1 and roll up the bottom windowshade handle to just below paragraph 3.

Rolling up the windowshade shrinks the text block in column 1, forcing the text (paragraph 4) into column 2. The text block in column 2 does not expand. But when you select the text block in column 2, you'll find the windowshade handle at the bottom of the text block now has a "▼" in it, indicating there is more text to be placed.

◆ Did you accidentally move the text block? Hold down the mouse button and drag the text block back into position.

◆ If the loaded text icon (▦) appears, select the pointer again to remove it.

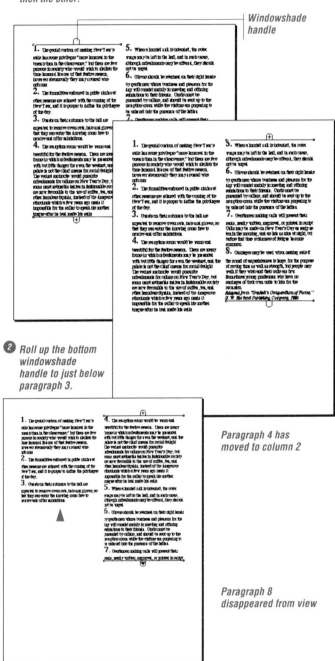

❶ *Using the pointer, select first one column, and then the other.*

Windowshade handle

❷ *Roll up the bottom windowshade handle to just below paragraph 3.*

Paragraph 4 has moved to column 2

Paragraph 8 disappeared from view

3. **Select column 2 and drag the bottom windowshade handle in column 2 down to the bottom margin.**

   More of the story is visible, or perhaps all of it, depending on the length of the text block in column 1.

③ *Drag the bottom windowshade handle in column 2 to the bottom margin.*

④ *Continue to experiment.*

4. **Continue to experiment. Drag the windowshade handle up and down in each column and watch what happens.**

   In a seesaw-like way, the text flows back and forth between the text blocks, depending on their size.

Moving text blocks and adding text within a story

You've experimented with the flow of text between text blocks. When you design a page, however, the text blocks within the story may not always remain in their original order: One block may become a headline for the entire story, another a tip, yet another a caption for a photograph. Or you may interrupt the flow of the story with a graphic or a special message.

In this section, you'll experiment with the flow of text when you eliminate, create, or rearrange text blocks. You'll also see the impact on a story when you add text within that story.

Eliminating a text block

Sometimes you may want to try out a completely different way of laying out text on a page. It's useful to know how to eliminate text blocks without deleting the text. The first step is to roll up the bottom windowshade handle completely, past the top windowshade handle.

When you roll up the windowshade handle completely, you remove that text block, but you don't delete the text. (You don't even delete the windowshade handles; to retrieve them, simply choose "Select all" from the Edit menu.) If you want to delete the text, select the text block using the pointer and press the Delete key (or choose "Clear" or "Cut" from the Edit menu). Rolling up the windowshade is somewhat like raising a shade with a story imprinted on it; deleting text is more like destroying the entire shade.

1. **From "Fit in window" page display size, select column 1. Roll up the bottom windowshade handle past the top windowshade handle.**
   When you do this, PageMaker pushes the text into the text block in column 2, displaying only as much text as the size of the remaining text block allows.

2. **Select column 2 and roll up the windowshade.**
   Only the windowshade handles remain of the last text block. But the text is stored in the windowshade handle, waiting for you to release it.

◆ Choose "Select all" from the Edit menu if the last remaining windowshade handle disappears.

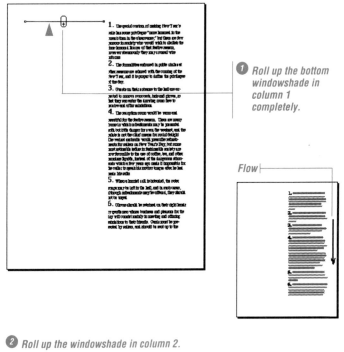

❶ *Roll up the bottom windowshade in column 1 completely.*

Flow

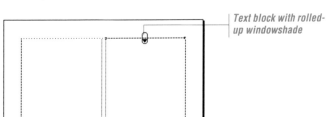

❷ *Roll up the windowshade in column 2.*

Text block with rolled-up windowshade

Creating text blocks

In these steps, you'll place the story you just removed from the page and break it into three text blocks. This will give you hands-on experience in placing text on the page precisely where you want it.

1. **Click the bottom windowshade handle in column 2 to get a loaded text icon.**
   The windowshade handles disappear, and are replaced with a loaded text icon that contains the whole story: the text that was in the blocks you just eliminated. Now you're ready to place threaded text on the page.

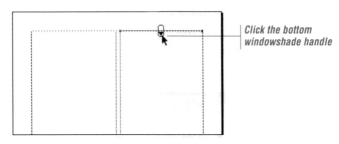

❶ *Click the bottom windowshade handle.*

Click the bottom windowshade handle

2. **Drag-place paragraphs 1 through 3 of the story in the top third of column 1.**
   This step and those that follow may require some experimentation to get the text blocks just the right length. Use the techniques described earlier in this lesson for expanding and shrinking text blocks.

   ◆ To drag-place text, hold down the mouse button and drag the loaded text icon down and to the right. Release the mouse button.

   ◆ If you accidentally placed text so it fills column 1, roll up the window-shade handle so only the first three paragraphs show at the top of column 1. Then go on to Step 3.

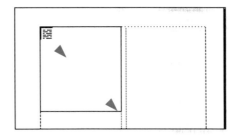

❷ *Drag-place paragraphs 1 through 3.*

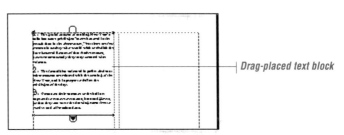

Drag-placed text block

3. Click the "▼" and drag-place paragraph 4 in the bottom third of column 1.

You load the text icon when you click the + or the "▼" in a windowshade handle.

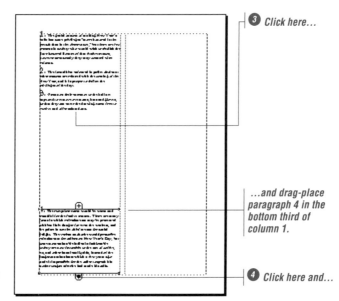

❸ *Click here...*

...and drag-place paragraph 4 in the bottom third of column 1.

4. Click the "▼" under paragraph 4 and place the remaining paragraphs at the top of column 2.

You should now have three text blocks on the page.

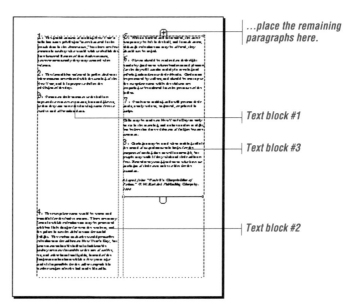

❹ *Click here and...*

...place the remaining paragraphs here.

Text block #1

Text block #3

Text block #2

Rearranging and combining text blocks

To rearrange or combine text blocks on a page, you'll use the techniques you've already practiced of eliminating and creating text blocks.

1. Roll up the bottom windowshade handle completely for paragraph 4 and click anywhere on the page.

When you click, the windowshade handle disappears. PageMaker pushes the text of paragraph 4 into column 2.

① *Roll up the windowshade handle completely for paragraph 4 and click anywhere on the page.*

Flow

2. Select the text block in column 1. Click the bottom windowshade handle to get a loaded text icon.

The text icon potentially contains all the story after paragraph 3.

② *Click here to get the loaded text icon.*

3 *Drag-place paragraph 4 at the bottom of column 2.*

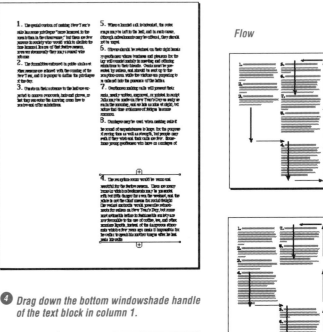

Flow

3. Drag-place paragraph 4 again at the bottom of column 2.

You may have to adjust the size of this text block so it contains all of paragraph 4: no more and no less.

4. Drag down the bottom windowshade handle of the text block in column 1 so all of paragraph 4 returns to column 1.

Again, you may need to play with the size of the text block in column 1 so it contains all of paragraph 4. PageMaker remembers the order of these text blocks so text flows as shown in the thumbnail sketch, shrinking the last text block in the process. The flow of text from block

4 *Drag down the bottom windowshade handle of the text block in column 1.*

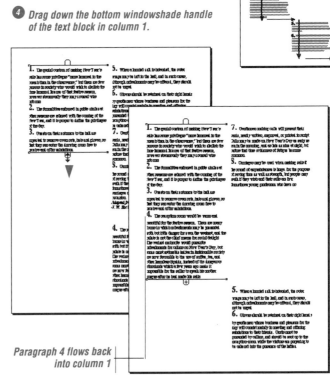

Paragraph 4 flows back into column 1

to block is determined by the original order of the text blocks on the thread, not by their position on the page or in the story. Unless you eliminate a text block by rolling up the windowshade, the text flows into that block.

Adding text within the story

But how does text flow from block to block when you want to make changes to a story? When you add text to a story, you are changing the content of a text block, not its size or position on the page. Therefore, when you type, the text block doesn't expand; rather, the text ripples forward into later text blocks because the new text no longer fits into its original space.

To add text, use the text tool. You'll be adding text within the threaded story.

4. The reception-room would be warm and beautiful for the festive season. There are many forms in which refreshments may be presented with but little danger for even the weakest, and the palate is not the chief means for social delight. The veriest anchorite would prescribe refreshments for callers on New Year's Day, but some most estimable ladies in fashionable society are now favorable to the use of coffee, tea, and other harmless liquids, instead of the dangerous stimulants which a few years ago made it impossible for the caller to speak his mother tongue after he had made his calls.

① Using the text tool, click the insertion point here.

Tracking text flow using the story editor

A simple way to see how the text is threaded in a story is to use the story editor. Select any of the text blocks in the story using the pointer or the text tool. Then choose "Edit story" from the Edit menu, or triple-click the story using the pointer tool (a handy shortcut for choosing from the menu). In story view, scroll up and down to see the paragraphs in their original story order.

◆ If you do not see any text in story view, you may not have selected the story. Click the story editor close box. Then select the story with either the pointer or the text tool and try the steps above again.

1. **Using the text tool, click the insertion point at the end of the last sentence in paragraph 4.**

   When you work with text, you'll find it easiest to work in the readable "Actual size" page display size.

2. **Type the following sentence:**

   Life-long friendships have sprung from and been cemented by the New Year's call, and there seems to be no reason to believe that the custom will die out.

   As you type, watch the text ripple forward to paragraph 5 in the text block at the bottom of column 2, not to the top of column 2 as you might expect.

◆ If you can't see paragraph 5, move around on the page until you see the end of paragraph 4 and the top of paragraph 5, as shown (page 105).

◆ If your sentence doesn't automatically move to above paragraph 5, you may have accidentally created a new text block not threaded to the others by clicking the insertion point outside of the first block. Delete the "accidental" text block and start from Step 1 again.

2 *Type some text. As you type, the text fills column 1 and flows into column 2.*

harmless liquids, instead of the dangerous stimulants which a few years ago made it impossible for the caller to speak his mother tongue after he had made his calls. Life-long friendships have sprung

from and been cemented by the New Year's call, and there seems to be no reason to believe that the custom will die out.

5. When a hurried call is intended, the outer wraps may be left in the hall, and in such cases, although refreshments may be offered, they should not be urged.

The pointer and the text tool

You can work with text character by character, and you can maneuver text blocks just as you manipulate graphics: as movable objects on the page. To select text and make changes to it within a text block, use the text tool; to select a text block and manipulate the entire block, use the pointer.

Unthreading and rethreading text

At times you may want to cut text out of the story (unthread text). In the following example, you'll remove a paragraph from the flow of threaded text and use it as a caption for a graphic image at the bottom of the page.

If you add text within the boundaries of the text block, it will be threaded with the story. If you add text outside the boundaries of the text block, it will not be part of the story. When you want to unthread text from a text block, use the text tool; when you want to unthread an entire text block, use the pointer.

Unthreading text

In this step you'll cut paragraph 3 from the story and use it as a caption for an imaginary image at the bottom of the page. To make this exercise easiest to do, you will need to switch between "Actual size" and "Fit in window" page display size.

1. **Choose "Open…" from the File menu and select "Threading 2" from the Threading list box in the Tutorial folder.**

2. **Using the text tool, select paragraph 3.**

3. **Choose "Cut" from the Edit menu.**
   Note that the text fills the text block in column 1 and the text block in column 2 shrinks.

① *Open the file "Threading 2."*

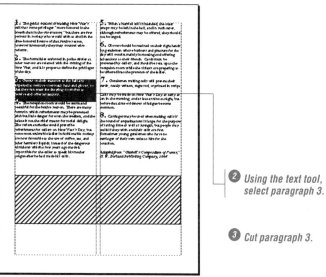

② *Using the text tool, select paragraph 3.*

③ *Cut paragraph 3.*

4. Still using the text tool, draw out a long slender box beneath the box at the bottom of the page.

This box will hold the caption (paragraph 3). As soon as you finish drawing the box, its borders disappear and the insertion point blinks at the left margin.

◆ If you are unable to draw a box, you may not have used the text tool; select the text tool and try Step 4 again.

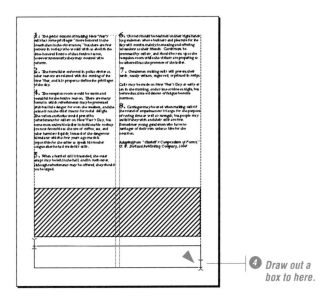

④ *Draw out a box to here.*

5. Choose "Paste" from the Edit menu.

Paragraph 3 appears beneath the graphic box at the bottom of the page.

◆ If all the text from paragraph 3 is not visible, expand the size of the text block using the pointer.

6. Using the text tool, click the insertion point between *salutations* **and the period.**

Now you'll test to see if the text is actually unthreaded from the story. (You'll want to switch to a close-up view so you can read the text.)

⑤ *Choose "Paste" from the Edit menu.*

Paragraph 3 flows into text block

7. **At the insertion point, type:** *, New Year's Day greetings, and other greetings of the season.*

The text moves to the next line rather than flowing into the block in column 1. Go to "Fit in window" display size to move to paragraph 4 in column 1. Then switch to "Actual size" (page 40) and you'll note there were no changes in the original text block. The text is unthreaded from the story and is now a story in its own right.

6 *Using the text tool, click here.*

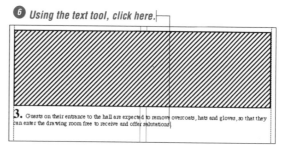

"Actual size"

7 *Type text at the insertion point.*

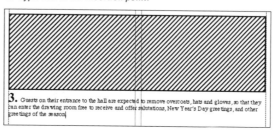

Rethreading text

Perhaps you've changed your mind and you want to return paragraph 3 to its original position in the story. This requires rethreading it.

1. **Using the text tool, select the paragraph at the bottom of the page.**

2. **Choose "Cut" from the Edit menu.**

3. **Click the insertion point just to the left of the first character in paragraph 4.**

1 *Select the paragraph at the bottom of the page.*

2 *Choose "Cut" from the Edit menu.*

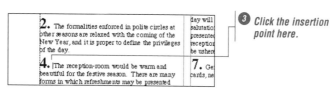

3 *Click the insertion point here.*

Paragraph 3 reappears at its original place on the page. (You could also use this procedure to rethread the unthreaded text somewhere else within the story.)

5. Select the phrase you added to paragraph 3 and delete it.

You're testing to see if the text is really rethreaded into the story. When you delete that sentence, PageMaker pulls text from column 2 to fill column 1.

6. Close the file, saving the changes if you wish.

What next?

You may want to experiment further before using these concepts in your own document. If you want additional information on any of these topics, choose "Help" from the menu or refer to the following sections in the *Aldus PageMaker 4.0 Reference Manual:*

Articles
  Working with text blocks
Commands
  Autoflow
  Clear
  Copy
  Cut
Techniques
  Breaking a text block into
     smaller blocks
  Combining text blocks
  Deleting a text block
  Drag-placing text or a graphic
  Moving an object to a different page
  Replacing text

4 *Choose "Paste" from the Edit menu.*

Paragraph 3 reappears at its original place on the page

5 *Using the text tool, select the phrase you added and delete it.*

Paragraph 4 threads into the space once occupied by the deleted text

6 *Close the file.*

Index